••• **Sue Ireland and Joanna Kosta**

PET
DIRECT

Student's Book

CAMBRIDGE
UNIVERSITY PRESS

Contents

Vocabulary	Language focus	Language booster
• hobbies and interests	• verbs of like and dislike	• *be keen on, be good at* and *be interested in*
• communication and technology	• present tenses	
• family, ages, describing people	• comparative and superlative adjectives	• extreme adjectives
• furniture and furnishings	• *so / such ... that* and *too / enough ... to*	
• daily life	• past simple and *used to*	
• in the city	• passive and active	• *owing to / due to*
• food and special occasions	• agreeing, disagreeing and suggesting	• *may / might / could*
• food and restaurant adjectives	• quantifiers	
• going to the doctor	• adverbs and adverbial phrases	• *should / ought to*
• compound adjectives	• *-ing* and *-ed* adjectives	
• travel and transport	• past continuous and past simple	
• the natural world	• conjunctions	• *despite / in spite of*
• sport	• comparative and superlative adverbs	
• feelings and opinions	• present perfect and past simple	• *for* and *since*
• school and study	• obligation, prohibition and permission	• past obligation and permission
• jobs	• relative pronouns	
• computers and technology	• predicting the future	
• weather	• first conditional and *unless*	• *going to*
• holidays	• second conditional	• *If I were you ...*
• music and festivals	• modal passives	
• clothes	• adjective order	• *like* and *just like*
• money	• *have / get something done*	
• cinema	• past perfect	
• reporting verbs	• reported speech	• reported questions
Vocabulary	Language focus	Language booster

Introduction

About *PET*

PET (Preliminary English Test) is an exam set by the University of Cambridge ESOL Examinations. If you pass, you will get a qualification which shows that you have an intermediate level of English and that you can:

- use English in a range of everyday situations with native or non-native speakers
- understand written texts from everyday life such as street signs and public notices, informal written notes and simple magazine and newspaper articles
- understand spoken English in a range of situations such as public announcements, information on the radio, and talks and interviews
- pick out factual detail and identify opinion and attitudes from longer reading and listening texts
- follow instructions and ask and answer questions appropriately
- express opinions and offer advice
- take part in a discussion and exchange factual information on familiar topics.

About *PET Direct*

PET Direct is a short intensive course which will help you improve your English, practise the question types used in *PET*, and develop the skills you need to pass the exam. There are 12 units in the book, each divided into two lessons. Each lesson looks at one of the topics that could appear in the exam, and contains Vocabulary, Language focus and authentic Exam practice.

Exam practice

Each lesson contains at least one exam task, so there are plenty of opportunities to practise every part of the exam. The exam tasks are supported by *Exam tips*, which give you helpful hints on how to do that task. There is also an *Exam guide* at the back of the book (pages 68 to 100), which describes each part of the exam in detail, gives an example for each part, and gives more hints and tips on how to approach the tasks. The *Workbook* contains lots more *Exam practice* questions and a complete practice test.

Language focus and Vocabulary

Each lesson introduces and re-uses important topic vocabulary. The *Language focus* sections systematically practise the key language areas you could need for the exam. There is also a *Language summary* section at the back of the book (pages 101 to 112), which looks at the language points covered in the lessons in more detail. You can get further practice of the language points and vocabulary in the *Workbook* and in the *Review* units.

The CD-ROM Exam Trainer

There are two ways you can use the CD-ROM. You can do a normal practice test under exam conditions, or you can use the *Exam Trainer* to get extra tips and advice for how to do each question. You can also print out your scores to see how you improve while you are studying.

Icons used in *PET Direct*

There is a list of the things you will practise in each lesson below the lesson title:

E = Exam skills
V = Vocabulary skills
L = Language skills

Each lesson also uses these icons:

 07 This is the track number on the Teacher's CD.

109 This is a page reference to the *Language summary*.

70 This is a page reference to the *Exam guide*.

The format of the exam

Reading and Writing Paper

This paper takes 1 hour and 30 minutes. It carries 50% of the total marks for the exam.

Part	Task format	Number of questions	Exam guide
Reading			
1	Read five short notices or messages and choose the correct answer to five questions.	5	p68
2	Match the requirements of five people to five of eight short texts.	5	p70
3	Read a text and decide whether ten statements are true or false	10	p72
4	Read a text and choose the correct answer to five questions.	5	p74
5	Choose the correct word to complete the spaces in a text.	10	p76
Writing			
1	Complete the second sentence so that it means the same as the first sentence.	5	p78
2	Write a short message including three pieces of information that you are given.	1	p80
3	Either: Write an informal letter answering some questions Or: Write a story using the title or the opening sentence given.	1	p82

Listening Paper

This paper takes about 30 minutes and carries 25% of the total marks. You hear each part twice.

Part	Task format	Number of questions	Exam guide
1	Listen to seven short recordings and choose the correct pictures.	7	p85
2	Listen to a talk or interview and choose the correct answers.	6	p88
3	Listen to one speaker and complete some notes.	6	p90
4	Listen to a conversation and decide if six statements are true or false.	6	p92

Speaking Paper

This paper takes about 10-12 minutes and carries 25% of the total marks. You do this part of the exam with one other candidate.

Part	Task format	Time	Exam guide
1	Answer the examiner's questions about you. Listen to your partner answering questions.	2-3 minutes	p95
2	With your partner, discuss possible options for a situation you are given, and decide what is best.	2-3 minutes	p96
3	Talk about the photograph you are given. Listen to your partner describing a photograph.	3 minutes	p98
4	Have a conversation with your partner, continuing the theme from Part 3.	3 minutes	p100

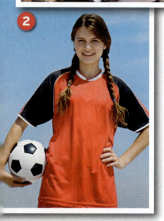

Reading

1 Read the online profile and match it to the correct picture above.

> Hi, I'm Zita and I love making new friends. I like books, fashion and playing the guitar. I hate Mondays and I can't stand going to the gym but I enjoy sports, especially athletics. I want to be a journalist and write about famous people.

Listening

02 **2** Listen to two students, Corey and Miki, talking together on their first day at college. Match the speakers to their pictures above.

3 Listen again and complete Corey's online profile.

> Hi, I'm Corey and I'm from **(1)** _____. In the winter I play ice **(2)** _____. In the summer I like mountain **(3)** _____ and playing **(4)** _____. I enjoy playing **(5)** _____ games but I hate **(6)** _____. If you want to look at my MySpace page, type in **(7)** _____.

Vocabulary: hobbies and interests

4 Read the profiles again and put the words connected to interests and free-time activities into the table.

interests	sport	computers	social activities
fashion			*making new friends*

101 ## Language focus: verbs of like and dislike

5 Read the sentences. Draw ☺☺, ☺, ☺, ☹ or ☹☹ next to each one to show the meaning.

0 *I hate Mondays.* ☹☹
1 *I can't stand going to the gym.*
2 *I quite like playing tennis.*
3 *I enjoy playing computer games.*
4 *We love going shopping.*
5 *I don't mind music stores.*

6 Complete the rule with two of the phrases from the box.

> the infinitive without *to*   the *-ing* form   a noun

After verbs of like and dislike we usually use _____ or _____.

7 How do you feel about these activities? Make sentences.

> chat online   play computer games with friends   play sports
> meet new people at parties   spend time on the computer
> talk about myself   wear fashionable clothes

I love playing sports, especially volleyball.

 Exam tip ✔68

- Do the questions one at a time as they are not connected to each other.
- Think about the purpose of the message. Is it an invitation, a request or a suggestion?
- Think about who is writing to whom.

Exam practice: Reading Part 1

8 Look at the text in each question. What does it say? Circle the correct letter A, B or C.

1

> **Tuesday's half-price day at the cinema. Let's go then instead of Friday. There'll be some new films but the one we're keen on will still be showing. OK? – Marc**

Marc wants to change
A the film they see.
B the cinema they go to.
C the day they see the film.

2

> Dan
> I can't open my emails! I know you're going out, so when Mel gets home from college can you ask her to sort the problem out?
> Mum

What should Dan do?
A ask Mel to come back from college to fix the computer
B explain the situation to Mel when she arrives home
C deal with Mum's emails before he goes out

3

> From: Luke
> To: Izzie
>
> Izzie
> You enjoy keeping fit don't you? My sister's got two tickets for a free session at Green's Gym. I've joined already, are you interested in going with her?
> Luke

A Luke is thinking of becoming a member of Green's Gym.
B Luke's sister has free gym tickets for Luke and Izzie.
C Luke wants Izzie to go to Green's Gym with his sister.

Exam practice: Speaking Part 1

Exam tip ✔95

- Don't just answer with one word – give reasons or examples.
- Try to avoid long silences. Say things like *well* while you are thinking.

9 In the first part of the speaking test the examiner will ask you some questions about your daily life and your likes and dislikes.
Ask your partner questions to complete the profile.

> First name: - - - - - - - - - - - - - - - -
> Last name: - - - - - - - - - - - - - - - -
> Home town: - - - - - - - - - - - - - - - -
> Hobbies: - - - - - - - - - - - - - - - -
> Other interests: - - - - - - - - - - - - - -
> Dislikes: - - - - - - - - - - - - - - - -

Writing

10 Write an online profile for your partner's webpage based on the information from Activity 9.

Keeping in touch

E Reading Part 5 · Writing Part 2 | V communication and technology | L present tenses

Vocabulary: communication and technology

1 How are these people keeping in touch? Match the words to the pictures.

> email __   landline __   mobile (phone) __   postcard __   text (message) __

2 Ask and answer the questions with a partner. Give reasons for your answers.

Which is the best way to

0 tell your friends a funny joke you've just heard?
1 find your friends at a crowded concert?
2 tell all your friends about an interesting website?
3 warn your friends you're going to be late?
4 tell your friends you're having a great holiday?
5 find out all your friends' news when you come back?

> *I think text or email is best because it's easy to send the joke to several people.*

3 Replace the underlined words with the correct forms of these verbs.

> click crash delete save surf

1 Ben's computer suddenly <u>stopped working</u> during the thunderstorm.
2 As soon as I've read my emails I <u>remove</u> them from the mailbox.
3 If you don't <u>store</u> the changes you make to a document you will lose them.
4 To start the program <u>press on the mouse</u> here.
5 You can spend hours <u>looking at different websites on</u> the internet.

Exam practice: Reading Part 5

4 Look at the article on page 9. Read the title and the text quickly but don't worry about the spaces. Who is Kimberley Brown and what is friendsforever.com?

5 Read the article again and circle the correct word for each space.

	A	B	C	D
0	**A** communicate	**B** contact	**C** write	**D** exchange
1	**A** Lot	**B** Many	**C** Much	**D** More
2	**A** delete	**B** email	**C** surf	**D** copy
3	**A** is	**B** was	**C** has	**D** are
4	**A** work	**B** rent	**C** employ	**D** apply
5	**A** form	**B** create	**C** think	**D** imagine
6	**A** prize	**B** hit	**C** success	**D** win
7	**A** last	**B** all	**C** least	**D** first
8	**A** local	**B** near	**C** close	**D** convenient
9	**A** need	**B** ought	**C** must	**D** may
10	**A** among	**B** for	**C** like	**D** with

Exam tip ✔76

• When you have chosen your answer read the whole sentence again to check it makes sense. Try the other options and decide why they are wrong.

FRIENDS FOREVER

Today thousands of young people **(0)** *communicate* with each other on social websites such as MySpace and Bebo. **(1)** _____ of them have web pages with background designs by Kimberley Brown. Anyone can **(2)** _____ these unusual and attractive designs from Kimberley's website, friendsforever.com, which **(3)** _____ quickly becoming one of the most popular sites on the internet.

17-year-old Kimberley already earns enough to **(4)** _____ her mother as her financial manager, and she is also training three former classmates to **(5)** _____ designs for her. Kimberley's parents and teachers are proud of her **(6)** _____ although they were shocked at **(7)** _____ when she gave up high school to concentrate on friendsforever.com.

Now however, Kimberley is studying for a degree at her **(8)** _____ college. She always refuses invitations to appear on radio or TV. 'I **(9)** _____ be a successful businesswoman,' she says, 'but at the moment I want to enjoy my free time with my friends, **(10)** _____ any other teenager.'

🔍 101 Language focus: present tenses

6 Read the examples. Are the underlined verbs in present simple or present continuous?

1 Kimberley already <u>earns</u> enough …
2 She <u>is training</u> three former classmates to help her.
3 She always <u>refuses</u> invitations to appear on TV.
4 At the moment I <u>want</u> to enjoy my free time.

7 Match the verbs in Activity 6 to the uses of the present tenses.

A present continuous for an activity happening now
B present simple for something that is generally true
C present simple for something that happens repeatedly
D present simple for a verb not usually used in continuous form, e.g. *hate, have (got), hear, know, like, remember, see, understand.*

I **(1)** _____ (spend) about 25 hours a month on the internet. Chat rooms are really popular but I **(2)** _____ (not understand) why. The conversations people **(3)** _____ (have) in them are usually really boring. I mainly **(4)** _____ (use) the internet for games. I **(5)** _____ (play) a fantastic game at the moment, called Free Rider. I **(6)** _____ (try) very hard to reach the next level.

Posted by: Ben Hilton

---

8 Complete the web-post with the correct forms of the verbs in brackets.

Exam practice: Writing Part 2

9 Match the verbs to the sentences they describe.

A remind   B apologise   C suggest   D offer   E explain   F invite

1 Sorry I forgot to text you last night.   B
2 You can borrow my old laptop until yours is mended if you like.   D
3 I can't talk with you now because I'm finishing an essay.   E
4 Don't forget to switch off the computer when you've finished.   A
5 Would you like to come to the internet café with me?   F
6 Why not join a social network like MySpace if you want to chat.   C

Exam tip ✔80

• Underline the verbs that introduce the three points to help you decide what to write.
• You only need to write 45 words so don't include unnecessary information.

10 You have a new computer. Write an email to your English friend, Alex.

In your email, you should
• explain why you like the new computer
• invite Alex to come to your house
• suggest what you can do together on the computer.

Write 35–45 words.

2.1 He's the youngest brother

E Reading Part 4 | V family, ages, describing people | L comparative and superlative adjectives

Vocabulary: family, ages, describing people

1 Look at the word box and answer the questions.

> bald   a beard   cheerful   confident   curly hair
> elderly   fair hair   glasses   a grandparent
> handsome   in his / her thirties   kind   lazy
> a moustache   pretty   shy   slim   tall   a twin

1 Which words can we use to describe people's:
   A personality   **B** age   **C** looks   **D** relationship?
2 Which words do we use with the verb *to be* and
   which with *to have*?
3 Describe one of the people in the pictures. Can
   your partner guess who it is?

Listening

🔊 03 **2** You will hear a man called Chris talking about his brothers, Steve
and Tim. What are the three brothers' jobs?

3 Are these sentences correct (A) or incorrect (B)?

		A: YES	B: NO
0	Chris is more hard-working than Steve.	☐	✓
1	Steve is the happiest of the three brothers.	☐	☐
2	Chris isn't as tall as Tim.	☐	☐
3	Chris is less good-looking than Tim.	☐	☐
4	Tim is already the most successful brother.	☐	☐

Language booster

extreme adjectives

Some adjectives already
mean *very ...* so we use
absolutely to make them
stronger.
We can use *really* with
both normal and
extreme adjectives.
*He's an absolutely brilliant
artist and his drawings are
really amazing.*

102 **Language focus:** comparative and superlative adjectives

4 Read the sentences in Activity 3. Write *C* by the ones that compare
two people and *S* by those that compare more than two people.

5 Complete the table and the rules.

	Adjective	Comparative	Superlative
0	one syllable	_____ + –er	+ the -est
1	two syllables ending in -y	y , + -ier	+ _____
2	two or more syllables	+ _____	+ _____

3 We use *as ... as* to say two things are **the same / different**.
4 We use *not as ... as* to say two things are **the same / different**.

6 Write sentences giving your opinion.

1 teenagers / elderly people / friendly
   I think teenagers are friendlier than elderly people because…
2 men / women / hard-working
3 shy people / confident people / attractive

- Some questions test attitude and opinion and some test specific detail, so read the question carefully.

Marie Davies – being a twin

When people hear that I'm a twin, their first question is always 'Can you and Paula read each other's thoughts?'

Being a twin means always having a best friend and never being lonely. From a very early age my sister and I both knew what the other was thinking and feeling. I've watched videos of us as young children, playing happily side by side, not needing to say anything. Sometimes even I can't tell which twin is which.

The teenage years are a difficult enough time for anyone, but they were even worse for us. At school I joined the basketball team, listened to hip hop music and dressed in sporty clothes, and Paula didn't want to know me. If I wore trousers, she wore a skirt. Her blonde hair was long and loose, while mine was dark and very short. Sometimes we had arguments, though they were quickly forgotten. Luckily we never liked the same kind of boyfriend! At 18, we went to different universities and didn't see each other for six months. When we met up again she seemed like a stranger.

Now we are both in our twenties and live 500 kilometres apart, though we speak or email most days. Our friends see us as individuals not twins. People who know us both say we're as different as night and day. Paula is shy and kind, and always forgetting things. I am more confident than she is and I've never forgotten a friend's birthday! Yet we both love painting, running and dancing and hate people who are rude or unkind! Underneath we are just as close as ever.

Exam practice: Reading Part 4

7 Read the text and questions below. For each question, circle the correct letter A, B, C or D.

1 In this text Marie Davies is
  A advising parents how to bring up twins.
  B describing her relationship with her sister.
  C explaining why she dislikes being a twin.
  D complaining about her friends' attitudes.

2 In films of their early childhood, Marie and Paula
  A play separate games.
  B behave in different ways.
  C communicate without speaking.
  D sometimes fight with each other.

3 What did Marie and Paula do at school?
  A They refused to copy each other's style.
  B They had long-lasting disagreements.
  C They liked to borrow each other's clothes.
  D They went out with the same boyfriend.

4 Marie thinks that she
  A has a better memory than Paula.
  B has more hobbies than Paula.
  C is more ready to trust people than Paula.
  D is less friendly than Paula.

5 What would the twins say about their lives?

A We were very close as children but we've never been as close since that time.

B We'd like to live nearer to each other – we've lost contact because our homes are so far apart.

C We had a lot of fun at secondary school – we looked so similar that the teachers often got our names wrong.

D Even though we lead separate lives now, there is still a very strong connection between us.

Writing

8 Complete the sentences about yourself and someone else in the class.

  1 This person is … 2 I'm more / less … 3 We both …

9 Read your sentences to the class. Can anyone guess who the other student is?

Vocabulary: furniture and furnishings

1 Look at the pictures. Which things can you see in each bedroom?

> armchair blinds carpet ceiling cupboard curtains cushion desk
> drawers duvet fan mirror pillow photos posters rubbish bin shelf

2 Which room is most similar to your room? How are these rooms different from yours?

3 Read the sentences. Which picture is each one about?

1 You can't relax here because the colours are so bright.
2 There are enough drawers to put things in.
3 There are so many posters that you can't see the wall.
4 The desk isn't big enough to do your homework on.
5 The ceiling is much too low to put up posters.
6 It's impossible to find anything in such a messy room.

102 Language focus: *so / such ... that* and *too / enough ... to*

4 Match the rules to the sentences in Activity 3.

A We use *so much* or *so many* with nouns.   _3_
B We use *so* with an adjective on its own.   _____
C We use *such (a)* with an adjective plus noun.   _____
D We put *too* before an adjective or adverb.   _____
E We can put *enough* after an adjective or adverb.   _____
F We can put *enough* before a noun.   _____

Exam tip ✔78

- In this part your spelling should be correct. Check your answers carefully.

Exam tip ✔85

- The speakers will talk about all the pictures but only one will be the right answer.

Exam practice: Writing Part 1

5 Here are some sentences about Akemi's new room. For each question, complete the second sentence so that it means the same as the first. Use no more than three words.

0 Akemi's family decided to move because their old house was too small.
Their old house wasn't *big enough* so Akemi's family decided to move.

1 Akemi's new room is bigger than her old one.
Akemi's new room isn't _____ her old one.

2 It had such dark walls that Akemi decided to paint them.
The walls were _____ dark that Akemi decided to paint them.

3 Akemi was too short to paint the ceiling herself.
Akemi wasn't tall _____ paint the ceiling herself.

4 The curtains were so ugly that Akemi threw them away.
They were _____ curtains that Akemi threw them away.

5 As there is plenty of space, Akemi's friends can stay the night.
There is _____ space for Akemi's friends to stay the night.

Speaking

6 Tell your partner which room in your house you like best, and which you like least. Give your reasons.

My least favourite room is the kitchen because it's so dark.

Exam practice: Listening Part 1

04 **7** For each question there are three pictures and a short recording. Choose the correct picture and put a tick (✓) in the box below it.

1 Where would the boy like to live?

 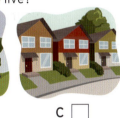

A ☐   B ☐   C ☐

2 What will the boy do on Saturday evening?

A ☐   B ☐   C ☐

3 Which computer desk does the boy have in his room?

A ☐   B ☐   C ☐

4 Which poster does the boy want?

A ☐   B ☐   C ☐

Speaking

8 Draw a plan of your room but don't draw any furniture in it. Give your plan to your partner.

Student A: Describe your room.
Student B: Draw the things in A's room.

Change over.

3.1 It used to be different

E Listening Part 4 • Speaking Parts 3 & 4 | **V** daily life | **L** past simple and *used to*

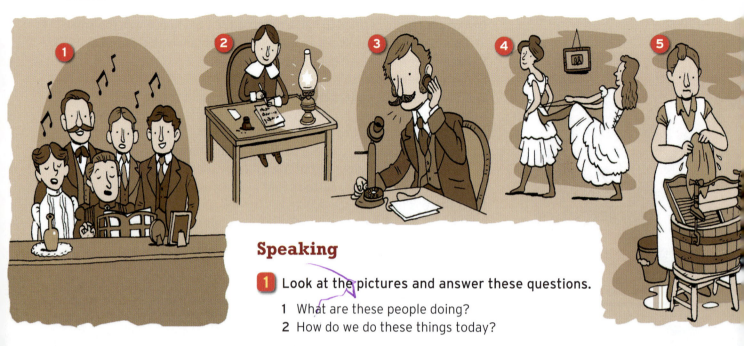

Speaking

1 Look at the pictures and answer these questions.

1 What are these people doing?
2 How do we do these things today?

Vocabulary: daily life

2 Match the verbs with the nouns by putting a tick (✓) in the box.

		house	bed	dinner	dishes	floor	housework	shopping	table	washing	washing up
clean		✓				✓					
do											
lay	the										
make											
wash											

3 Talk to your partner. Who usually does these jobs in your family? Who did these things yesterday? How similar are your families?

Exam tip ✓92

• Read the instructions and questions to get an idea of the topic and the speakers' opinions.

Exam practice: Listening Part 4

4 🔊 05 You will hear a conversation between a boy, Carl, and a girl, Jennie, talking about writing an essay on life a hundred years ago. Decide if each sentence is correct (A) or incorrect (B).

	A: YES	B: NO
1 Carl found writing the essay difficult.	☐	☐
2 Jennie thinks that people had a healthier diet a hundred years ago.	☐	☐
3 Jennie is shocked to learn about the clothes young boys wore.	☐	☐
4 Jennie admires the way people entertained themselves.	☐	☐
5 Carl and Jennie agree that children were more respectful in the past.	☐	☐
6 Jennie is grateful to Carl for helping her with the essay.	☐	☐

Living in the Past

Tonight the popular TV show *Living in the Past* returns to our screens with the Willensdale family, who will be 'living' in the 16th Century for a month. How will they survive life in the past? Perhaps the Hatters can give them some tips.

In the last series, the Hatter family **(0)** *lived* for a month exactly like families used to do in 1900. This is what they said about the experience.

🔍 **103 Language focus:** past simple and *used to*

5 Read the examples and complete the rules about the past.

*I **finished** my essay last night.*
***Did** everybody **use to eat** like that?*
*Little boys **used to wear** dresses.*
*They **didn't have** washing machines or vacuum cleaners,*

1 We use past simple for single events that are **finished / still going on**.
2 We use *used to* for a past **habit / single event** that no longer exists.
3 *Used to* is followed by **past simple / the infinitive.**
4 To form past simple of regular verbs, add **-(e)d / -ing** to the infinitive.
5 We form negatives with **not / did not** and the infinitive.
6 We form questions with **do / did** plus the infinitive.

6 Complete the article with verbs from the box, using *used to* or past simple. If both are possible, use *used to*.

> get up   have to   ~~live~~   look   play   take   wash   watch   wear

Mrs Hatter (aged 45): It was terribly hard work. All month, I **(1)** _____ before everyone else to light the fire and heat the water. In 1900 people **(2)** _____ all their clothes by hand, which took at least a whole day. The first time I tried, it **(3)** _____ me three days!

Mr Hatter (aged 47): I **(4)** _____ wear old-fashioned clothes all the time like the ones they **(5)** _____ in 1900. I **(6)** _____ really odd and people stared at me on the bus when I went to work!

Mark Hatter (aged 14): Before I went on the programme, I **(7)** _____ lots of TV but they didn't even have electricity in 1900. People **(8)** _____ card games or read by oil lamp, so that's what we did too. It was fun, actually!

Exam practice: Speaking Parts 3 and 4

 **Exam tip** ✓ 98

Speaking Part 3
• Say who the people are, where they are and what they are doing. Don't just list everything you can see.

7 The examiner will give you and your partner each a photograph to talk about for around a minute. Look at the photographs on page 62 and take turns to listen to each other.

🔊 06 **8** Next, the examiner will ask you to talk together about a topic connected with your photographs. For example:

> *Your photograph showed families doing things together. Now, I'd like you to talk together about the things you do with your family now, and the things you used to do with them when you were younger.*

Exam tip ✓ 100

Speaking Part 4
• Talk to your partner, not the examiner. Take turns, ask questions and react to what your partner says.

Listen to two students, Dimitri and Elena, talking about the topic. Which of these things do they do with their families now? Which did they use to do?

> do homework   do housework   eat meals
> go on holiday   play sport   watch sport

9 How do they start the conversation? Does one of them say more than the other? How do they involve each other?

The street is lined with trees

Vocabulary: in the city

1 Match the photos to the cities.

Moscow __ New York __ Paris __ London __

2 Complete the words. How many of the places are in the pictures?

0 Sports events and concerts are held here.   s _tadium_
1 This is where ships are loaded and unloaded.   p _ _ _
2 This tall building may stand alone or be part
   of another building.   t _ _ _ _
3 Markets or events are often held in this
   open space.   s _ _ _ _ _
4 Cars and motorbikes are not allowed here.   p _ _ _ _ _ _ _ _ area
5 This electric train network runs under
   some cities.   u _ _ _ _ _ _ _ _ _ _
6 This model of an important person is usually
   placed where everyone will see it.   s _ _ _ _ _

Exam tip ✔72

• The questions will be in
the same order as the
information in the text.

Exam practice: Reading Part 3

3 Look quickly at the text on page 17. Is it from an encyclopedia, a travel
guide or a school geography book? How do you know?

4 Look at the sentences below about Montreal. Read the article to
decide if each sentence is correct (A) or incorrect (B).

		A: YES	B: NO
1	Visitors can enjoy free entertainment on the streets of the old city centre.	☐	☐
2	It is possible to visit the Old Port by car.	☐	☐
3	Mount Royal Park is situated on the edge of the city.	☐	☐
4	Some of the trees in the park were planted in 1998.	☐	☐
5	Sporting events are held in the Olympic Stadium all year round.	☐	☐
6	Visitors to the Biodome will discover the natural history of four different areas.	☐	☐
7	Some people have homes in the Underground City.	☐	☐
8	Lunchtime is a good time to look around the Underground City.	☐	☐
9	You will find *The Illuminated Crowd* on the ground floor of the BNP tower.	☐	☐
10	Festivals take place throughout the year in Montreal.	☐	☐

What to see in Montreal

There are plenty of things to do in French-speaking Montreal, Canada's second largest city!

Old city centre and port
The narrow streets of the historic city centre are lined with museums and restaurants. There are also lively squares with street artists, musicians and other performers. Major attractions include the City Hall, the Old Customs House and the Old Port, which has become a year-round playground for tourists and local people, with ice-skating and ice-sculpture competitions. Most people come by underground, owing to the limited amount of parking available.

Mount Royal Park
In the centre of this enormous park is the mountain that gives the city its name. It's easy to forget you are in the heart of a huge city when walking across one of its well-signposted tracks. There's a small lake, an exhibition centre and a forest. Many of the trees had to be replaced owing to storm damage in 1998. The park is open from sunrise to sunset.

Olympic Stadium and Biodome
When this stadium was built for the 1976 Olympic Games, its architecture was considered extraordinary. These days the stadium is mainly used for concerts and conferences, with occasional football matches during winter months. The former cycling track is now the Biodome, a science centre and ecological mini-zoo. Four different environments, including the rainforest and the Arctic, are recreated here and visitors can experience the climate, wildlife and plant-life of those regions.

Underground City
Due to the city's extreme temperatures, Montrealers have developed the world's largest underground pedestrian network. Citizens are protected from both the heat of summer and the freezing winter temperatures by five underground train stations linked by over 30 kilometres of walkways with 1,600 shops, 200 restaurants, 34 cinemas and 1,600 apartments. The best time to visit in order to avoid the crowds is between 9 and 11 a.m. and 2 and 4 p.m.

BNP tower and *The Illuminated Crowd*
This striking glass office tower is best known for the amusing statue, *The Illuminated Crowd*, outside its entrance. A life-size group of adults and children are shown, all pointing in amazement at something passers-by cannot see. This curious artwork is photographed by thousands of tourists every week.

Festivals
Whatever your interest – jazz, comedy, cinema, theatre, sport – Montreal has a festival for it. And with over 162 festivals on the calendar, there's a good chance there will be one going on no matter when you choose to visit.

---

(103) Language focus: passive and active

Language booster

owing to / due to

These words have a similar meaning to *because of*. They are followed by a noun.

Due to the extreme temperatures, Montrealers have developed an underground network.

Most people come by underground owing to the limited amount of parking.

5 Look at the examples and complete the rules by choosing the correct word in the sentences below.

Active: *People use the stadium for concerts.*
Passive: *The stadium is used for concerts (by people).*

1 We use **passive / active** sentences when we do not know or it is not important to say who does the action.
2 To make passive sentences we use *do / be* in the correct tense and the **infinitive / past participle** of the verb.
3 If we need to say who does the action, we use *by / of*.

6 Complete the sentences about Montreal. Use the active or passive in the correct tense.

1 In 1852, much of the city / destroy / a large fire.
2 In the 1960s and 70s many old buildings / repair.
3 Old Montreal / declare / a historic district in 1964.
4 In 1998 an ice-storm / cause / $1 billion worth of damage to the city.
5 Many famous films / make / in Montreal.
6 66% of Montrealers / speak / French as their first language.

Speaking

7 You each have some information about the history of London. Ask your partner the questions to complete the information.
Student A, look at page 64. Student B, look at page 66.

Review 1

1 Unscramble the underlined letters in the first half of this article to make words for members of the family.

An ancient tennis ball

Nobody knew that there was a tennis ball on the roof of Lincoln Cathedral except the family of the boy who put it there.

Almost 100 years ago Gilbert Bell and his **(0)** brerhto *brother* used to play outside the cathedral, near their **(1)** frahet's bread shop. One day the ball landed on the cathedral roof and was never seen again.

The story became part of the Bell family history. Gilbert's 78-year-old **(2)** neweph David told his **(3)** crihlned and **(4)** drangcrihlned about it. Whenever they visited Lincoln they used to check to see if the ball was still there. When David's **(5)** nso, Christopher, got married he even took his new **(6)** fiew to see it.

2 Put the verbs in the second half of the article in the active or passive form of present or past simple.

Then one day Christopher **(0)** *visited* (visit) the Christmas Market in Lincoln and **(1)** _____ (see) workers repairing the roof. As a joke, he **(2)** _____ (write) a letter to the cathedral staff and **(3)** _____ (ask) to have the ball back. 'If it **(4)** _____ (find) you can have it,' they replied. So far, however, there has been no sign of it.

The ball **(5)** _____ (believe) to be one of the oldest in the UK. The earliest tennis ball in the London Tennis Museum **(6)** _____ (make) in 1916, so Gilbert Bell's is probably even older.

3 Match the nouns to the verbs.

a bath   the bed   breakfast   a chat
the cooking   the dinner   fun   your homework
the housework   a mess   a mistake
the shopping   the washing-up

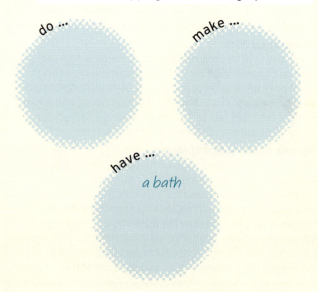

do ...

make ...

have ...
a bath

4 When you were ten years old, which of these did you use to do? Which do you do now?

buy comics   eat a lot of sweets
go on holiday with your friends
have a mobile phone   have your own bedroom
play computer games   support a football team

Compare your answers with your partner's.
A: *Did you use to buy comics, Wiktor?*
B: *Yes, I did. I used to buy one every week.*
A: *Do you still buy comics?*
B: *No, I don't. Now I buy football magazines.*

Make six sentences about yourself and your partner.
Wiktor used to buy comics but now he buys football magazines.
I didn't use to .... but now I ....

5 Read this information posted on the internet by Li Chen and choose the correct word.

Hi! My name is Li Chen and I (0) **am living / live** in Beijing. Beijing is the capital of China and it (1) **changes / is changing** all the time. When my mother was young, everyone (2) **travelled / travels** around by bicycle, and there was far (3) **less / little** traffic. Now the traffic is very (4) **heavier / heavy**. Also, people used to (5) **live / living** in single-storey houses but most of these (6) **are / were** pulled down and replaced by (7) **absolutely / very** enormous apartment blocks, office buildings, and department stores. This city (8) **grows / is growing** very fast, but there are still (9) **many / more** historic places to visit, such as the Forbidden City, and the Temple of Heaven. I think living in Beijing is (10) **absolutely / very** exciting.

6 Complete these mini conversations using *so, such, too* or *enough*.

1 Have you tidied your room yet?
   Sorry, I've been ___*too*___ busy.
   Well, will you do it tomorrow?
   I won't have _____ time tomorrow either.

2 It's _____ lovely weather. Shall we have lunch in the garden?
   I don't think it's warm _____ yet to eat outside.

3 I didn't know it was _____ far to the old town. Shall we get a taxi?
   It's _____ expensive, the bus is cheaper.

4 I like your new room. I didn't know you had _____ many posters.
   I've got _____ many really. There isn't _____ space on the walls for them all.

On target?

How well can you do these things?	☆	☆☆	☆☆☆
E use grammar and vocabulary knowledge to complete a text			
E write a short communicative message			
E find and understand information in a text			
E listen for key information			
E describe a photograph and discuss a connected topic			
V talk about myself, my family and my home			
L use the present simple and present continuous tenses			
L use comparative and superlative adjectives			
L use the simple past tense and *used to*			
L understand and use the passive voice			

E Exam skills   V Vocabulary skills   L Language skills

4.1 Shall we have a party?

E Writing Part 3 (letter) • Speaking Part 2 | V food and special occasions | L agreeing, disagreeing and suggesting

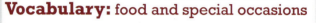

Vocabulary: food and special occasions

1 Match the pictures to these words.

bread roll __   chocolate cake __   fried fish __   green salad __   lemon tart __
roast chicken __   spinach omelette __   strawberries and cream __

2 Discuss these questions with your partner.

1 What's your favourite food? How often do you eat it?
2 What kind of food do you usually have:

at a birthday party   at a picnic   in a restaurant   on New Year's Eve

104 Language focus: agreeing, disagreeing and suggesting

07 3 You will hear three short conversations. Write the number of the conversation next to the correct description.

Choosing a present ___   Deciding how to celebrate ___   Planning a menu ___

4 Read the phrases from the conversations above. Do we use them to agree (*A*), to disagree (*D*) or to suggest (*S*)? Add ideas of your own.

Let's …	*S*	*Yes, you're right.*	___
That's a good / the best idea	___	*How / What about …*	___
Well, I'm not sure …	___	*What a good idea!*	___
I don't think that's a good idea.	___	*Why don't we …*	___
I think we should …	___		

5 Complete the second conversation with the phrases.

we should   shall we   let's   I don't think   you're right

A: It's Mum and Dad's wedding anniversary next month, isn't it? **(1)** _____ organise a party for them?
B: Oh, **(2)** _____ that's a good idea. Dad hates parties. And anyway, I haven't got time. I need to study for my exams.
A: Hm. **(3)** _____. It's too much work. **(4)** _____ just take them out to a restaurant.
B: Yes, that's the best idea. **(5)** _____ book it soon!

08 6 Listen again and check your answers.

Language booster

may / might / could

Use these modal verbs to talk about possibility.
I might get him a computer game.
He could already have that one.

- Begin with *Dear* or *Hi* and the person's name.
- End with a phrase like *See you soon*, *Take care* or *Best wishes*.

Exam practice: Writing Part 3 (letter)

7 Read the exam question and the answer to it. Does the answer:

1 have a suitable beginning and ending?
2 answer all the questions in Philip's letter?
3 have enough words?
4 include only important information?

8 Write your own answer to the question.

- This is part of an email you receive from your friend Philip.

> I want to organise a party for my parents' 20th wedding anniversary. Would a surprise party be best, or is that a bad idea? Should I book a table at a restaurant or have the party at home? What would you do?

- Now write an email, answering your friend's questions.
- Write your email in about 100 words.

Hi Philip,

Thanks for your email. I went to a great party last night. It was my friend Sam's 18th birthday. The food was fantastic and there was a band playing too. For your parent's party, I think you should book a table at a restaurant. Invite lots of guests and make sure they are all there when you arrive with your parents. I don't think it is a good idea to have the party at home.

- Talk about the advantages and disadvantages of all the pictures.
- Take turns to ask questions and give your opinion.

Exam practice: Speaking Part 2

09 9 Listen to two people doing this exam task and answer these questions.

1 How many of the pictures do they talk about?
2 Does one person talk more than the other?
3 Do they just give their opinion or do they give reasons as well?

> A friend of yours is organising an end of year party for her class. Talk together about the different ideas, and decide which one is the best. Here is a picture with some ideas to help you.

10 Read the exam question again and try the task with your partner.

You'll be given a lot to eat!

E Reading Part 2 | **V** food and restaurant adjectives | **L** quantifiers

a relaxed atmosphere

a stylish restaurant

Vocabulary: food and restaurant adjectives

1 Which of the adjectives can describe these things: *food*, *service*, *atmosphere* and *restaurant*? You can use words more than once.

bitter	creamy	delicious	disgusting	excellent
fashionable	lively	modern	relaxed	salty	simple
slow	smart	stylish	traditional	unfriendly

Listening

2 What's most important to you in a restaurant: fast service; tasty food; low prices; great atmosphere?

10 3 Listen to Vanessa telling Kath about a visit to a restaurant called *Charlie's*. Are these sentences true (A) or false (B)?

	A: YES	B: NO
1 Kath went to *Charlie's* once last year.	☐	☐
2 The restaurant was very quiet when Vanessa went there.	☐	☐
3 Vanessa enjoyed her main course, but not the starter or dessert.	☐	☐
4 There were very few waiters in the restaurant.	☐	☐
5 Vanessa complained to the manager about her meal.	☐	☐

(104) Language focus: quantifiers

10 4 Complete the sentences from the listening with the correct quantifier from this list. Listen again to check your answers.

a couple of	a few	a great deal of	all of	few	little	a lot of
many	most	much	no	none of	plenty of	several	some

1 I went there _____ times last year.
2 I always had _____ fun.
3 I saw _____ famous people.
4 There was _____ atmosphere at all.
5 There were _____ waiters.
6 _____ them wanted to serve us.

5 Which quantifiers are used with countable nouns, which with uncountable nouns, and which can be used with both?

6 Put the quantity expressions in order from least to most.

0% ━━ *few* ━━━━━━━━━━━━━━━━━━━━━━━━━━━━━━━ 100%
little

7 Talk in groups about restaurants where you live. Whose neighbourhood offers the best restaurants?

There are a couple of great Chinese restaurants near me …

Exam practice: Reading Part 2

8 The people on the left all want to go to a restaurant. On the right, there are eight restaurant reviews. Decide which restaurant would be the most suitable for the following people.

1 Claudia is organising her 18th birthday party. She wants to go to a <u>fashionable</u> restaurant run by a <u>top chef</u>, where she and her friends can <u>dance</u> after their meal.

2 Sonia and Emilia work in the city centre and would like to have lunch near their office. They want a restaurant that can serve good quality meals quickly.

3 James would like to take his mother to a quiet restaurant for lunch. He has plenty of time and isn't worried about the price, as long as the food and service are excellent.

4 Pete and Ella would love to go somewhere where they can eat outside. They don't want to spend a great deal of money, and would enjoy listening to live music.

5 Carlos wants to go out in the evening to a lively restaurant with a group of friends. They like eating large meals but are not keen on complicated cooking methods.

Restaurant reviews

http://www.restaurantreviews.com

A Manzo
The famous John Allerton is a truly great chef. He uses traditional ingredients but puts them together in surprising new ways. The dining room is small and noisy though, and the prices are sky high! Manzo is just a few kilometres from the city and is open for both lunch and dinner every day.

B Café on the Hill
This restaurant is only open in the evening and serves traditional French food at very reasonable prices. The cooking is good, but you don't get much on your plate. There are several tables in the garden, and a band plays every night.

C Riva Riva
This fun, busy restaurant serves simple Italian food in a modern setting. Cinema screens in the dining room show old films and loud music is played from the speakers. Make sure you are hungry, because you will be given a lot to eat! Open from 7 p.m. til midnight.

D Coral Blue
Whether you want a relaxed dinner or a nightclub with the best DJs in town, smart and stylish Coral Reef provides it all under one roof. The restaurant has won many prizes for its modern menu, designed by head-chef Antoine Lefevre, who is known throughout the industry.

E The Sun and Moon
This restaurant is in the heart of the business district and is ideal if you're short of time in the middle of the day. It's busy and noisy, and expensive, but you never have to wait long for your meal. The chef uses the freshest ingredients and the service is fast. It is not open in the evening.

F Tosca
If you have something to celebrate, Tosca is the place to go. The atmosphere is amazing, with live music and dancing until late. There is a bar serving snacks and light refreshments, but most people come for the music rather than the food.

G The Olive Tree
It's very unusual to find a restaurant in the middle of the city where you can eat outside, but The Olive Tree has a beautiful garden where you can do just that. Prices are reasonable and the food is good, but unfortunately the waiters are rather unfriendly.

H Starlings
The atmosphere here is calm and peaceful and the food is delicious. The waiters will look after you beautifully although the chef may keep you waiting – he's famously slow! It costs more to eat here than at other city centre restaurants, but it is worth it. Open between 11.30 a.m. and 3 p.m.

Speaking

9 Imagine you and your partner each went out to a different one of these restaurants last night and had a terrible time. Complain to each other about your restaurant. Whose experience was worse?

5.1 It's terribly painful

E Listening Part 1 | V going to the doctor | L adverbs and adverbial phrases

RECEPTION

The doctor says _____

HEALTH CENTRE

Language booster

should / ought to

We use *should* and *ought to* when we are giving advice.
You should have an X-ray.
You ought to go home and lie down.

Exam tip ✔85

• Read the question carefully and look at the pictures before you listen. Think about the words you might hear.

Vocabulary: going to the doctor

1 Who says what? Mark statements 1–9 patient (**P**) or doctor (**D**).

P 1 I hope I haven't broken my ankle. It's terribly painful.

___ 2 I've got a really sore throat and a nasty cough.

___ 3 Open wide and I'll have a look.

___ 4 I'll give you a prescription for some painkillers. You should take one tablet three times a day.

___ 5 You ought to go home and lie down, and you shouldn't eat anything for 24 hours.

___ 6 I've cut myself. It's still bleeding.

___ 7 I've got stomach-ache and I feel sick.

___ 8 I've got earache and a temperature.

___ 9 I'll put a bandage on it for you.

___ 10 You should have an X-ray.

2 Match the statements to the people in the pictures. There is one statement you won't need.

3 You and your partner both have health problems. Give each other advice. Student A, look at page 64. Student B, look at page 66.

Exam practice: Listening Part 1

4 For each question there are three pictures and a short recording. Choose the correct picture and put a tick (✓) in the box below it.

1 What has the tennis player injured today?

A ☐   B ☐   C ☐

2 What should the girl stop doing?

A ☐   B ☐   C ☐

3 Where will Rosie go tomorrow?

A ☐   B ☐   C ☐

4 What happened to Molly on holiday this year?

A ☐   B ☐   C ☐

Reading

5 Look at the headline and the photo. What do you think happened? Read the text. Were you right?

Shark attacks boy in his bedroom

A shark attack in a bedroom miles from the sea may sound unbelievable, but that is what happened to 14-year-old Sam Hawthorne. Mrs Hawthorne was woken <mark>suddenly</mark> by loud screams <mark>from Sam's room</mark> <mark>in the middle of the night</mark> and thought Sam was having a bad dream. When she <mark>nervously</mark> went to check, she found the shark's teeth had stuck <mark>firmly</mark> <mark>in Sam's cheek</mark> and there was blood on his pyjamas from the wound.

Sam had <mark>accidentally</mark> sleepwalked into the jaws of a long-dead souvenir shark that was hanging on his bedroom wall. Luckily the teeth did not go <mark>near his eye</mark>, but he is likely to have a scar. Sam needed a day off school <mark>afterwards</mark> to recover from his accident. "Most students say the dog has eaten their homework. My excuse was I have been bitten by a shark." The school <mark>officially</mark> recorded the reason for his absence as 'shark attack'.

6 Are these sentences correct (A) or incorrect (B)?

	A: YES	B: NO
1 The Hawthorne family live on the coast.	☐	☐
2 Mrs Hawthorne woke up when Sam sleepwalked into her room.	☐	☐
3 Sam didn't go to school on the day after the accident.	☐	☐

(105) Language focus: adverbs and adverbial phrases

7 Divide the highlighted words and phrases from the article into:

    1 Adverbs of manner (tell us how)
    2 Adverbs of time (tell us when)
    3 Adverbs of place (tell us where)

8 Complete the rules.

    1 Adverbs of manner usually go **before / after** the verb.
    2 If there is more than one adverb the order is usually

      ☐ → ☐ → ☐

9 Add the words on the right to Mrs Hawthorne's letter to Sam's teacher. There may be more than one correct place for some words.

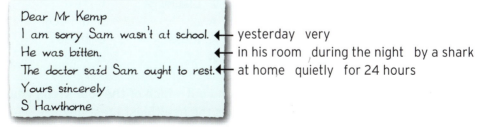

Dear Mr Kemp
I am sorry Sam wasn't at school. ← yesterday very
He was bitten. ← in his room during the night by a shark
The doctor said Sam ought to rest. ← at home quietly for 24 hours
Yours sincerely
S Hawthorne

10 Make adverbs from the adjectives.

    angry happy noisy polite quick quiet rude slow

11 Talk about one of the topics in the manner of one of the adverbs above. Your partner must guess which adverb you chose.

    my pet an accident the internet my town TV stars my family

5.2 Exercise needn't be boring

E Reading Part 5 | **V** compound adjectives | **L** -ing and -ed adjectives

Exam practice: Reading Part 5

1 Read the article quickly and match the pictures to the correct steps.

Step 1: Try to eat a wide variety (0)____A____ different foods. You can do this easily by increasing the (1)_____ of fruit, vegetables, whole grains and freshly-squeezed juice in your diet. These foods will (2)_____ you against disease and ageing.

Step 2: (3)_____ the quantity of sugary and high-fat food in your diet. Because this kind of food (4)_____ so good, it's easy to eat too much of (5)_____. Remember, for long-lasting benefits, you should make these changes permanent.

A four-step plan for healthy living

Step 3: (6)_____ more exercise. Exercise needn't be boring. (7)_____ yourself to a five-kilometre run or to learn an unusual sport. Don't worry (8)_____ you can't afford to join a gym – (9)_____ are plenty of low-cost options, such as jogging, and you'll feel relaxed afterwards.

Step 4: Be kind to yourself! Don't get too tired and make sure you (10)_____ enough sleep. This is the key to a healthy, stress-free life.

2 Read the article again and circle the correct word for each space.

0 **(A** of)	B for	C by	D to
1 A sum	B amount	C size	D total
2 A save	B hold	C protect	D support
3 A Sink	B Fall	C Drop	D Reduce
4 A tries	B eats	C tastes	D pleases
5 A them	B it	C theirs	D yours
6 A Make	B Perform	C Practise	D Do
7 A Challenge	B Test	C Force	D Push
8 A if	B although	C whether	D since
9 A those	B these	C here	D there
10 A fall	B take	C have	D go

Exam tip ✔ 76

• Read the whole text once before you try to answer the questions.
• Look at what comes before and after the space to help you decide which word fits best.

3 Find out which of the four steps your classmates already do. Who has the healthiest lifestyle?

Vocabulary: compound adjectives

4
> **compound adjective** *n.*
> an adjective made with two or more words joined together with a hyphen

Which word in the title of the article is a compound adjective? Underline six more compound adjectives in the article.

5 Match the pictures to the descriptions.

1 a low-fat cake _____
2 a star-shaped cake _____
3 a chocolate-covered cake _____
4 a half-eaten cake _____

6 Use one word from box A and one from box B to make compound adjectives. Complete the phrases below in as many ways as you can.

A: badly highly long low recently two well

B: broken cost fat kilometre lasting opened qualified run

1 a _____ ankle
2 _____ changes
3 a _____ diet
4 a _____ sports centre
5 _____ staff
6 a _____ race

105 **Language focus:** *-ing* and *-ed* adjectives

7 Look at the examples from Activity 1 and complete the rules with *-ing* or *-ed*.

Exercise needn't be boring.
You'll feel really relaxed afterwards.
Don't get too tired.

1 _____ adjectives describe people or situations.
2 _____ adjectives describe how they make you feel.

8 Complete the text with an adjective form of the word in brackets.

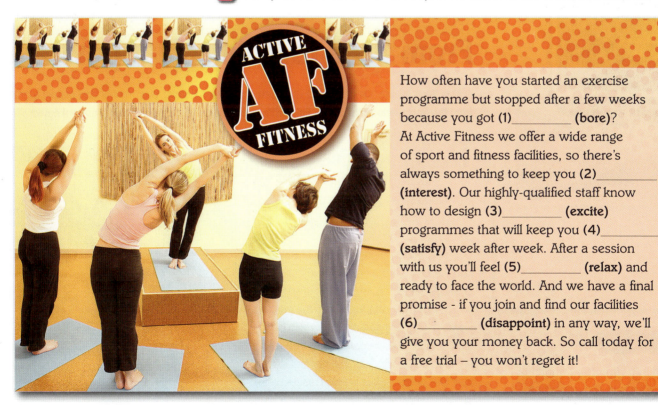

How often have you started an exercise programme but stopped after a few weeks because you got (1)_____ (bore)? At Active Fitness we offer a wide range of sport and fitness facilities, so there's always something to keep you (2)_____ (interest). Our highly-qualified staff know how to design (3)_____ (excite) programmes that will keep you (4)_____ (satisfy) week after week. After a session with us you'll feel (5)_____ (relax) and ready to face the world. And we have a final promise - if you join and find our facilities (6)_____ (disappoint) in any way, we'll give you your money back. So call today for a free trial – you won't regret it!

Speaking

9 Role-play joining a health club. Student A, look at page 64. Student B, look at page 66.

6.1 The wind was blowing hard

E Reading Part 3 | V travel and transport | L past continuous and past simple

Vocabulary: travel and transport

1 Match the words to pictures A–G.

> (aero)plane __   bicycle __   boat __   bus __
> car __   dog sled __   train __

2 Match each group of words to one of the ways of travelling.

0 to sail / cabin / deck / voyage *boat*
1 to take off / check-in / flight / baggage
2 to cycle / seat / brakes / helmet
3 to board / carriage / platform / announcement
4 to pull / snow / ice / luggage
5 to catch / traffic / passenger / route
6 to overtake / seat belt / windscreen / fuel

Exam practice: Reading Part 3

3 Read the title of the article about two young men who travelled from the North to the South Pole. Look at the map of their route and read the first sentence. What means of transport do you think they used on their journey?

From Pole to Pole – Manpowered

In May 2008, at the age of 20, Rob Gauntlett and James Hooper became the first people to travel from the North Pole to the South Pole without engines or motors, using only natural power.

They set off for the North Pole from Qaanaaq in Greenland on April 8th 2007. They began their journey on skis, but their progress was so slow that after a few weeks they changed to dog sleds. It was on this part of the journey that Rob almost lost his life. They were racing over the ice when Rob dropped his glove into the snow. As he was running back to get it, he fell straight through the ice into the freezing water, hitting his head as he fell. He lay face down in the water for three minutes until James was able to pull him out. 'It was four hours before he was rescued and taken to hospital,' explained James. 'Our parents wanted us to give up at that point, but we knew we had to continue.'

After their three-month trek on foot across the Arctic, Rob and James sailed from Upernavik in Greenland to New York. There they began a 17,000-kilometre bike ride through Central and South America to Punta Arenas in Chile. Some of their best memories are of this part of the trip. 'We cycled 160 kilometres a day, which was tiring, but every night when we stopped, people met us with big smiles and offered us food!'

Exam tip ✓72

- Underline the important words in the sentences and text as you read.
- Check the sentences and text again. Make sure they say the same thing.

4 Read the text to decide if each sentence is correct (A) or incorrect (B).

	A: YES	B: NO
1 Many travellers have completed this journey without powered transport.	☐	☐
2 Rob and James changed to dog sleds in order to improve their speed.	☐	☐
3 Rob's accident in the Arctic happened because he fell off the dog sled.	☐	☐
4 Rob managed to climb out of the water alone.	☐	☐
5 Rob and James had to wait for several hours before help arrived.	☐	☐
6 The boys' parents persuaded them to continue with their journey.	☐	☐
7 People in South America were very friendly to Rob and James.	☐	☐
8 Both Rob and James were on deck when the storm hit their boat.	☐	☐
9 James was knocked off the boat during the storm.	☐	☐
10 Rob and James are confident that they will go on another journey together.	☐	☐

106 **Language focus:** past continuous and past simple

5 **Look at the diagram. Which verb is in past continuous and which is in past simple?**

⟵ *They were racing over the ice ...* ⟶

▲ *... when Rob dropped his glove.*

6 **Complete the rules with *past continuous* or *past simple*.**

A We use _____ to talk about completed actions in the past.

B We use _____ to talk about activities in progress at a particular point in the past. We often link two activities with *while*.

C We use _____ to talk about a longer activity interrupted by a shorter action. We use _____ for the shorter action.

Find four more examples of past continuous in the article. Do they match rule B or rule C?

7 **Complete the sentences with the correct form of the verb in brackets.**

Last week I **(0)** *had* (have) a nasty accident. I **(1)** _____ (ride) my bike when I **(2)** _____ (hit) a stone and **(3)** _____ (fall off). Luckily I **(4)** _____ (wear) a helmet. I **(5)** _____ (try) to stand up but my leg **(6)** _____ (hurt) too much. A young man **(7)** _____ (clean) his car nearby and he **(8)** _____ (see) the accident. He **(9)** _____ (go) inside to call an ambulance. While we **(10)** _____ (wait) he **(11)** _____ (make) me a cup of tea. We **(12)** _____ (start) chatting and **(13)** _____ (find out) that we used to go to the same school. We **(14)** _____ (still talk) when the ambulance **(15)** _____ (arrive) half an hour later.

Speaking

8 **Tell your partner a story. It can be true or invented. Choose a title.**

A nasty accident   An exciting adventure   A terrible journey

- **Use past continuous to set the scene and give background details.**
  Who were the people in your story? What were they doing?
- **Use past simple to tell the main events of the story.**
  What did the people do? What happened in the end?

Your partner must guess if the story is true or made up.

Finally the boys boarded their 107-metre yacht for the voyage across the Southern Ocean. But just four days before they reached the South Pole, a huge storm almost swept James into the sea. 'I was working on the deck while Rob was trying to sleep below. The wind was blowing at about 100 kph and the waves were rising 25 metres into the air. Suddenly a huge wave crashed into the boat. I wrapped my arms around a pole and held it tightly. The boat turned over on its side, but luckily when it came back up again I was still holding on.'

They finally sailed into Sydney Harbour, Australia, 396 days after setting off. Now back in the UK, the pair are working on a book and a documentary about their experiences. 'We don't have plans for another expedition just yet, but I'm sure we will one day. It's just a matter of time!'

6.2 Into the rainforest

E Listening Part 2 • Writing Part 3 (story) | **V** the natural world | **L** conjunctions

Vocabulary: the natural world

1 Match the plant and wildlife words to the picture.

> branch __   bush __   butterfly __   cat __   crocodile __   flower __
> giraffe __   insect __   leaf __   monkey __   parrot __   polar bear __
> snake __   tree __   whale __   zebra __

Exam tip ✔88

- The questions will be in the same order as the information in the recording.
- Read the questions before you listen so that you know what kind of information you are going to hear.

2 Which of the animals don't belong in the rainforest? Where do they live?

3 Which of these places have you visited? Ask your partner about his / her experiences.

> a cave   a cliff   a desert   a forest   a lake
> a mountain   a rainforest   a waterfall

Exam practice: Listening Part 2

🔊12 **4** You will hear a radio interview with an explorer, Sally Brendle. For each question, put a tick (✓) in the correct box.

1 On her last trip, Sally
  A found a new kind of snake. ☐
  B saw a rare crocodile. ☐
  C discovered an unknown river. ☐
2 When Sally was a child she
  A enjoyed going to the zoo. ☐
  B worried about the environment. ☐
  C kept wild animals at home. ☐
3 What work did Sally do when she went to Africa?
  A She helped to build a school. ☐
  B She studied animals in the forest. ☐
  C She recorded the numbers of certain animals. ☐

4 Sally was invited to join the Amazon expedition because
  A she knew a lot about medicine. ☐
  B one of the original team members was injured. ☐
  C she was a well-known plant expert. ☐
5 What does Sally say about the rainforest?
  A It's a dangerous place. ☐
  B It's very calm. ☐
  C It's easy to get lost. ☐
6 Sally's new TV programme is about
  A some less well-known animals. ☐
  B the ways people can protect wildlife. ☐
  C her experiences in the rainforest. ☐

30

106 Language focus: conjunctions

5 Read the sentences and put the underlined words into the table.

When Sally was a child she kept wild animals at home.
Sally was invited to join the Amazon expedition _because / since / as_ she knew a lot about medicine.
Even though / Although the snake was tiny, it was still very exciting.
Many animals will disappear _unless_ they are protected.

Time (tell us when)	Condition (tell us what might happen)	Reason (tell us why)	Contrast (link two different ideas)
when			

Language booster

despite / in spite of

We use _despite / in spite of_ + noun to introduce two contrasting ideas.
Despite the heat and the wildlife, it's quite safe.

6 Find sentences with these conjunctions in the transcript of Sally's interview on page 116, and put the conjunctions into the table.

although   as soon as   but   if   (in order) to   since   so   while

7 Complete the spaces in the blog with these linking words.

although   although   ~~as soon as~~   as soon as   because
before   but   so that   until   when   while

http://www.myblog.com

A fun adventure

My friends and I set off on our trip to the waterfall **(0)** _as soon as_ it was light. We cycled for an hour **(1)**_____ we reached the edge of the forest. We locked our bikes **(2)**_____ no one could take them and continued on foot. **(3)**_____ it was very hot we were all wearing long trousers **(4)**_____ there were so many insects. **(5)**_____ we reached the waterfall we put on our swimming things and jumped in.

We had fantastic fun **(6)**_____ the water was freezing cold. Then we had our picnic. **(7)**_____ we were eating we saw some beautiful butterflies among the trees. Soon it was time to go. **(8)**_____ we left we picked up all our rubbish. It was getting dark **(9)**_____ we finally arrived home. We were very tired **(10)**_____ it was a great day.

Exam tip ✔82

- Before you start, plan your story carefully.
- Use conjunctions to connect the ideas.
- Make sure it comes to a natural end.

Exam practice: Writing Part 3 (story)

8 Look at the exam task and plan your story. Think about:

1 where the story is set
2 what the discovery is – a plant, an animal, a building, something else
3 who the characters are in the story
4 what happens at the beginning, middle and end of your story.

- Your English teacher has asked you to write a story.
- Your story must have the following title:

  An amazing discovery

- Write your story in about 100 words.

9 Write your story.

10 Read your story to your group. Whose is the most exciting / original?

Review 2

1 Match each of the words in the box to one of the lists below.

car   diet   flight   main course   rainforest   ~~restaurant~~   taste   unwell   wound

0 atmosphere	service	menu	price	*restaurant*
1 sweet	sour	delicious	fruity	
2 baked potato	roast chicken	fried fish	spinach omelette	
3 bandage	blood	cut	pain	
4 earache	temperature	sore throat	cough	
5 sugary	high-fat	healthy	meat-free	
6 announcement	board	baggage	check-in	
7 traffic	windscreen	overtake	seat belt	
8 insects	waterfall	trees	monkey	

2 Read the restaurant review and circle the correct adjectives.

An evening to remember

Last night I had an extremely **(0)** *entertained /* (entertaining) evening at Kenji, the new Teppanyaki restaurant on Feltbury High Street. Teppanyaki is a traditional Japanese way of cooking, in which the chef prepares and cooks the food right there in front of you.

The chefs are very skilled and it's **(1)** *amazed / amazing* to watch them work. They make a real show of it – ours even started juggling with his knives, which was a bit **(2)** *frightened / frightening*. One or two of the chefs are also comedians. Ours kept us **(3)** *amused / amusing* all evening. The food was very fresh and beautifully cooked.

The atmosphere of the restaurant varies depending on where you sit. At the front, it's very lively and noisy. But there are a couple of tables at the back where you can have a quiet meal.

I do have one or two small complaints. Some of the people in our party were vegetarians and they were a bit **(4)** *disappointed / disappointing* to find there were so few dishes on the menu for them. Also, although the service was friendly, there weren't really enough waiters. We had to wait ages to get our drinks. But none of us complained as we were feeling so **(5)** *relaxed / relaxing* and happy. I can highly recommend a visit to Kenji's – you'll have an evening to remember.

3 Read the review again and choose the correct quantifier for the sentences below.

0 The writer (had a lot of) */ didn't have much* fun at Kenji.
1 *All / Some* of the chefs at Kenji are very funny.
2 There are *a few / a lot of* quiet tables in the restaurant.
3 The writer has *no / a couple of* complaints about Kenji.
4 There's *not much / a great deal of* vegetarian food on the menu.
5 There *are plenty of / aren't many* waiters in the restaurant.

4 Complete the mini-conversations by putting the verbs into past simple or past continuous.

1 A: How / be / your journey? *How was your journey?*
  B: Terrible! They / repair / the roads and the traffic was awful.
2 A: I / eat / a meal in a restaurant the other day when I / find / an insect in my soup!
  B: That's disgusting! What / you / do?
  A: I / scream / and / call / for the waiter!
3 A: I / try / to call you last night but you / not answer / your phone. What / you do?
  B: I / jog. I'm trying to get fit.
4 A: How / hurt / your leg?
  B: I / not look / where I / go / so I / fall / into a hole in the pavement.

5 Here are some things an explorer said in a TV interview.
Complete the sentences with the words in the box.

| although as soon as because if ~~in order to~~ so |

0 'I'm here in this African forest *in order to* try and save the
wildlife of the region.'

1 '_____ the conditions are difficult, it's very enjoyable work.'

2 '_____ we arrived we set up our equipment and began our
research.'

3 'Time is running out for some of these animals _____ we
need to hurry.'

4 'It's difficult work _____ the forest is very thick and there
are few roads.'

5 '_____ we are lucky, we may discover a new species.'

6 Complete the conversation. What does David say to Sally?

Sally: Look! We've received an invitation to my old school
friend's wedding in France! I'd love to see her again.
Shall we go?

David: **(0)** _D_

Sally: We don't have to fly. We could drive. That way we'll be
able to see more of the country.

David: **(1)**_____

Sally: I'd forgotten. How about taking the train?

David: **(2)**_____

Sally: Why don't we take a day or two off work then? We could
have a little holiday while we're there.

David: **(3)**_____

Sally: Oh, I love Paris. It'll be beautiful at that time of year.

David: **(4)**_____

Sally: Yes. I can't wait!

A: Oh, I don't think that's a good idea.
You know I get car sick on long
journeys.

B: Shall I book the tickets then?

C: That's not a bad idea, but it's still a
lot of money for just one day's trip.

D: Well, I'm not sure. Can we afford to
fly to France?

E: What a good idea! It's ages since we
last went away. What about going
to Paris?

On target?

How well can you do these things?	☆	☆☆	☆☆☆
E write a longer text			
E find important information in several short texts			
E listen for key information			
E scan a text for specific information			
V talk about food and healthy living			
V talk about travel and the natural world			
L make suggestions and agree and disagree with other people			
L use adverbs and adverbial phrases correctly			
L use past continuous when telling a story			
L join ideas with appropriate linking words			

| E Exam skills   V Vocabulary skills   L Language skills |

7.1 I could easily swim further

E Reading Part 2 | V sport | L comparative and superlative adverbs

Vocabulary: sport

1 Match the sports to the pictures.

> athletics __ cycling __ fencing __ football __ golf __ hockey __
> horse-riding __ karate __ rock-climbing __ running __ shooting __
> snowboarding __ swimming __ tennis __ windsurfing __

2 🔊 13 You will hear an interview with Kirsty Muir, an athlete, about training for the modern pentathlon. Which sports does she talk about?

3 Listen again and complete Kirsty's training timetable.

9.30	10.30	12.00 lunch	1.30	3.00	3.30	6.30	7.30 exercises

4 Put the sports from Activity 1 in the correct column.

go...	play...	do...
swimming		

Language focus: comparative and superlative adverbs

5 Read the sentences and choose the correct ending to the rule.

I could easily swim further.
Shooting's the sport I enjoy the least.

We use comparative and superlative adverbs to compare
people or things / the way people do things.

6 Look at the triathlon results table and complete the sentences using comparative or superlative forms.

	Cycling	Swimming	Running	Total
Kirsty	2 points	2 points	3 points	7 = Gold
Ludmila	1 point	3 points	2 points	6 = Silver
Helene	3 points	1 point	1 point	5 = Bronze

1 Kirsty ran _____ (well) than she usually does but she didn't swim _____ (fast).
2 Ludmila cycled _____ (badly) than Kirsty and Helene but she did the _____ (well) in swimming.
3 Helene ran _____ (slow) than the other two but she tried _____ (hard).

Exam practice: Reading Part 2

7 The people below all want to learn a new outdoor sport. Underneath, there are eight descriptions of short courses in outdoor sports. Decide which course would be the most suitable for the following people.

3 Marie is a non-swimmer who has not done any exercise for a long time. She loves speed and wants to try a new activity for half a day.

1 Juan wants to spend half a day learning a water sport that he can do when the waves are not big enough for surfing. He dislikes being part of a group.

2 Claire would like to try climbing but is nervous about heights. She doesn't want to spend much money to start with.

4 Lech, Monika and their twelve-year-old daughter are all confident swimmers. They'd like to learn a new water sport on a half-day course.

5 Peter and his eighteen-year-old son Dan want to spend a day together doing a range of outdoor activities that they will find challenging. They also hope to see some wildlife.

Sports courses

A Swindale Beach
Learn respect for the sea by booking a place on this two-hour ocean knowledge session. Basic life-saving and sea safety techniques are covered, making it an excellent introduction for anyone of 14 or over planning to take up water sports.

B Portloebar
When the sea's too rough for sailing, try land yachting. In a taster session lasting three hours you will first learn to stop and turn by using the sail: land yachts have no brakes or steering wheel and can reach 50 kph! This beach sport is fast and fun and requires little fitness.

C Ramsey Rocks
On this exciting six-hour adventure, you will climb over cliffs and rocks and jump from them into the sea. You can explore sea caves and you'll see a variety of birds and other creatures. A professional guide is responsible for the safety of the six group members at all times. Minimum age 16.

D Carliport Island
On this one-day sea outing with qualified instructors, you first learn the basics of how to control your boat. You will then sail round the island, stopping for a picnic lunch at one of the island's many hidden beaches. Dolphins and seals are often seen.

E Boulder Crags
We offer one-day introductory courses to this challenging rock-climbing activity. It is done without safety ropes, just a few metres off the ground and so is suitable for children. Only climbing shoes are needed, as helmets and a thick landing mat are provided.

F Lasham
Learn the absolute basics of traditional rock-climbing in a day on this fun course. No experience is required but you must be prepared to work hard to reach the top. We recommend you wear climbing shoes and waterproof trousers and jacket. Groups will be kept small.

G Glaze Lake
This calm lake is the ideal venue for beginners of all ages to learn to windsurf. If, after our four-hour taster lesson you are unable to sail your board, we will give you back your money! Teaching groups are according to age and ability with a maximum of six members.

H Whitesands
In this brand new activity from the US, you stand on a six-metre long board and use a large paddle. This allows you to ride waves when the sea's too calm to use your regular surf board. You'll need strength, surfing experience and good balance for one of our individual two-hour lessons.

Speaking

8 Make questions from the prompts and talk to your partner about the sports in the texts above.

1 You / ever / try / any of these activities?
2 Which / like / do / most? Why?
3 Which / like / do / least? Why?

He has just won first prize

Rahul wins National Spelling Bee

For the past five years the Hathwar family have travelled to Washington DC to watch their children in the top US spelling competition, the National Spelling Bee. Their elder daughter, Gayathri, has taken part since she was nine years old, and her younger brother Rahul has just won the first prize of $40,000 at his first attempt.

Rahul and Gayathri studied hard to reach the final, which was shown on television all over the US. Mr Hathwar helped his children beforehand by making lists of words and checking their meanings. He was confident they would do well. Rahul even stopped playing computer games and doing his other hobbies to concentrate on learning spellings. 'I don't regret it,' he says. 'The Spelling Bee has taught me to work hard. I didn't expect to come first so I was amazed at the result. I was so anxious when I arrived at the Television Centre I couldn't stop shaking.'

Gayathri admits she is a little disappointed that she has never won a prize but she is very proud of her brother's success.

Reading

1 How do you think the boy is feeling? What do you think he has done to win this cup? Read the newspaper article and check.

2 Are these sentences true (A) or false (B)?

	A: YES	B: NO
1 Gayathri and Rahul have each been in the Spelling Bee the same number of times.	☐	☐
2 Rahul is sorry he gave up his hobbies for the Spelling Bee.	☐	☐
3 Rahul was very nervous before he went on television.	☐	☐
4 Gayathri feels jealous because her brother has won the prize.	☐	☐

Vocabulary: feelings and opinions

3 Find words in the article that are used to mean:

upset   surprised   certain   nervous   pleased

Use each new word in a sentence about yourself.

*I was **disappointed** when our team didn't win the football last week.*

🔍 107 Language focus: present perfect and past simple

4 Match the sentences to the rules.

1 *Gayathri has taken part since she was nine years old.*

2 *Rahul has just won the first prize.*

3 *Mr Hathwar helped his children beforehand.*

4 *She has never won a prize.*

A We use past simple for something that happened at a definite time in the past.

B We use present perfect (often with *just*) for something that happened in the recent past.

C We use present perfect (often with *yet, already, never* or *ever*) for something that happened at an indefinite time in the past.

D We use present perfect (often with *for* or *since*) for something that started in the past and is unfinished.

Language booster

for and since

- We use *for* with a period of time.
  For the past five years …
- We use *since* with a definite time or a time clause.
  … since she was nine years old.

5 Complete the sentences with either past simple or present perfect of the verb in brackets.

1 After the final of the Spelling Bee, the family _____ (go) to a restaurant to celebrate.
2 As soon as Rahul _____ (arrive) home he _____ (switch) on his computer and _____ (start) playing computer games.
3 Rahul's head teacher _____ (display) the cup in the school entrance hall so everyone can admire it.
4 Rahul _____ (not decide) yet how to spend the prize money.

Exam practice: Listening Part 3

🔊 14 6 You will hear some information about a competition. For each question, fill in the missing information in the numbered space.

Exam tip ✔90

- If you don't hear the answer the first time, go on to the next question. You will hear the recording twice.
- Try to spell your answers correctly.

Design a book cover competition

Name of book:	(1) _____
Judges:	Jacquie Cooper and her (2) _____, Suzie Wilson
Design the cover:	by computer or by hand
	do not use (3) _____
Size:	20 x 13 centimetres
Include:	small (4) _____, title and author's name
First prize:	(5) _____ with Jacquie Cooper
Closing date:	Wednesday (6) _____

7 In pairs, decide what the most important part of this competition is:

A an original idea   **B** a beautiful image   **C** following the instructions.

Exam practice: Writing Part 2

Exam tip ✔80

- Don't write more than 45 words.
- Be sure to include the three points but don't write any unnecessary information.

8 Read the exam task and one student's answer.

Which point is not included? Which piece of information is not necessary? Correct the six spelling errors in the answer.

You have won two tickets for a sports event.

Write a note to an English friend of yours. In your note, you should

- explain how you got the tickets
- tell your friend what the event is
- invite your friend to go with you.

Write 35–45 words.

Hi George
I'm writting to tell you some good news. I've got two tikets for the match between Liverpool and Everton on Wedensday. Do you want to come whit me? I think we will enjoi it. I've got an intresting new computer game.
Sam

9 Write your own answer to the question.

Speaking

10 Plan a spelling competition for your classmates.

8.1 Students don't have to study!

E Reading Part 1 | **V** school and study | **L** obligation, prohibition and permission

Vocabulary: school and study

1 Work in pairs to match the groups of words to their headings. Can you add any more words to each group?

1 punishment / rule / permission
2 corridor / classroom / laboratory
3 essay / project / homework
4 degree / certificate / diploma
5 university / college / school
6 take / pass / fail
7 lessons / timetable / subjects
8 Biology / Geography / Science

A places in a school
B qualifications
C school curriculum
D places to study
E tests and exams
F school subjects
G controlling students' behaviour
H school work

2 Read the article about an unusual school. Student A, look at page 65. Student B, look at page 67. Complete the text by giving each other clues for the missing words.

3 Are these sentences about the school correct (A) or incorrect (B)?

	A: YES	B: NO
1 Students <u>don't have to</u> do any homework.	☐	☐
2 Students <u>needn't</u> study at all.	☐	☐
3 Students <u>have to</u> decide for themselves how they spend their time.	☐	☐
4 Students <u>can</u> go shopping during the day.	☐	☐
5 Students <u>must</u> do three chores every day.	☐	☐
6 Students <u>mustn't</u> miss the school meetings.	☐	☐
7 Students from this school <u>can't</u> go to university.	☐	☐

4 Work in pairs to write down as many advantages and disadvantages of this kind of education as you can think of.

108 **Language focus:** obligation, prohibition and permission

5 Complete the rules with the underlined words from Activity 3.

1 It's not necessary: _____ and *needn't*
2 It's necessary: _____ and _____
3 It's forbidden: _____ and _____
4 It's allowed: _____

Language booster

past obligation and permission

The past of *must* and *have to* is *had to.*
I had to work things out for myself.
The past of *can* is *could.*
I could do it in my own time.

6 Rewrite the school rules so that all sentences start with *We*. Sometimes there will be more than one right answer.

0 All students must wear full school uniform at all times.
   We have to wear full school uniform at all times.
1 Don't drop litter in the playground.
2 All mobile phones must be switched off.
3 It's not necessary to call school when you are ill. Send a letter the next day.
4 Don't bring MP3 players into school.

7 Work in pairs to write three rules for your ideal school. Compare your list with another pair. Did you have the same ideas?

Exam practice: Reading Part 1

8 Look at the text in each question. What does it say? Circle the correct letter A, B or C.

All items of lost property will be thrown away at the end of term.

Year 9 – You don't need a packed lunch for Friday's trip to Beecham Valley, but don't forget your raincoats. A maximum of £5.00 spending money each please! We will return at 4.45 p.m.

Jane – I just booked some tickets for my parents for the school show and there are only a few left. If you want yours to come you'd better hurry!
Sophie

Students from Year 12 are free to use the library computers at any time.

1 The purpose of this notice is to
   A ask students to check their classrooms for items of lost property.
   B tell students where to go to collect items of lost property.
   C warn students to collect their lost property soon.

2 This message is telling students
   A what they need to bring with them on the trip.
   B what time they must arrive at school on the day of the trip.
   C how much they have to pay for the trip.

3 A Jane should order some tickets as soon as possible.
   B If Jane wants to see the show she needs to book a ticket.
   C Jane needn't get any tickets because Sophie has enough.

4 What does this notice say about Year 12 students?
   A They needn't pay to use the library computers.
   B They don't have to get permission to use the computers.
   C They must check whether the computers are free before they use them.

Speaking

9 Discuss the sentences below with your partner. Write A beside the sentence if you agree with your partner and D if you disagree.

1 Nothing is more important in life than a good education. ____
2 You don't have to make a child learn. Children *want* to learn. ____
3 You don't need a degree to do well in life. ____
4 School uniforms are a bad idea. ____
5 Most schools have far too many rules. ____
6 Homework is more important than school work. ____

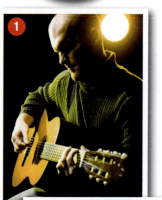

Vocabulary: jobs

1 Match the jobs to the pictures.

actor __   basketball player __   chef __   flight attendant __
football coach __   journalist __   musician __   scientist __

2 Which of the jobs is the most interesting / exciting / dangerous / stressful? Which is the best / worst paid? What qualifications, training or experience might you need to do each job?

Exam practice: Listening Part 2

3 Look at the exam task. Read questions 1–6 and all the options. What is Sandy's job?

> You will hear a woman called Sandy talking to a group of students about her job. For each question, put a tick (✓) in the correct box.

Exam tip ✓88

- You have 45 seconds to read the questions before you listen.
- The correct answer will have the same meaning as the recording but may use different words.

🔊 15 **4** Listen to Sandy and answer the questions.

1 What did Sandy Duffy want to be when she was at school?
  A a journalist ☐
  B a musician ☐
  C a basketball player ☐

2 What did Sandy study at university?
  A Maths and Physics ☐
  B Film-making ☐
  C Art ☐

3 How did Sandy get her first job as a video game writer?
  A She answered a job advertisement. ☐
  B She met someone at a conference. ☐
  C She sent some information about herself to a company. ☐

4 What does Sandy like best about being a video game writer?
  A the prizes she has won ☐
  B the high salary ☐
  C the people she works with ☐

5 What does Sandy dislike about being a video game writer?
  A She has to travel a lot. ☐
  B She has to work long hours. ☐
  C She often has to change her job. ☐

6 Sandy says that people who want to be video game writers should
  A write stories from an early age. ☐
  B try and get a job as soon as they leave school. ☐
  C make sure they get a good education. ☐

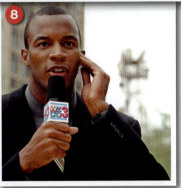

(108) Language focus: relative pronouns

5 Look at these examples from the listening.

1 I had an accident <u>when</u> I was playing basketball.
2 I went to film school, <u>where</u> I studied lighting and special effects.
3 I had a friend <u>whose</u> job was organising conferences.
4 She met a man <u>who</u> owned a company.
5 He owned a company <u>that</u> made video games.

6 In which sentence does the relative pronoun refer to

A a thing   _5_   *that* / which
B a time   ___   _____
C a possession   ___   _____
D a place   ___   _____
E a person   ___   _____

7 What kind of job do you think this advert is for? Read and check. Then fill each space with a relative pronoun. Sometimes there is more than one possible answer.

Are you interested in science? Do you love working with children? Do you want a part-time job (0) *that / which* **you will enjoy and have fun doing? If so, read on!**

Cool Science is a company **(1)** _____ aim is to give young people a better idea of what science is all about. We provide fun, entertaining activities for children **(2)** _____ are aged between 4 and 11.

You will be an instructor and your role will be to give exciting science demonstrations in schools, clubs, and at special events such as parties.

You will be able to choose **(3)** _____ you work – evenings, weekends or during the day. We will try to find you work close to **(4)** _____ you live.

We need people **(5)** _____ personal qualities suit this kind of work – experience is not necessary as full training will be given.

Send us a CV and letter of application today!

Writing

8 In pairs, write a job advertisement for one of the following jobs.

   dog-walker sports instructor waiter babysitter shop assistant

9 Read other students' job adverts. Which one would you apply for?

Speaking

10 Role-play a job interview. In pairs, choose one of the jobs from Activity 8. Student A, interview Student B for the job.

Student A: Would you employ Student B?
Student B: Would you take the job?

Change roles.

9.1 We will have robots

E Reading Part 3 | V computers and technology | L predicting the future

Vocabulary: computers and technology

1 Complete the questions with the words in the box.

> chips   digital   interactive   network   program   remote control   software

1 Do you have a _____ camera?
2 Do you know how to write a computer _____?
3 Have you got anti-virus _____ on your computer?
4 Do you know how to connect two or more computers to make a _____?
5 Do you know what all the _____ in your computer do?
6 Who is usually in charge of the TV _____ in your family?
7 Do you enjoy going to museums with _____ exhibits?

2 Ask and answer the questions with your partner.

Exam practice: Reading Part 3

3 Look at the picture and describe it with a partner. Which things do you think we will all have in our homes in 20 years' time? Read the article once to check.

4 Read the sentences below about the house of the future. Read the text again to decide if each sentence is correct (A) or incorrect (B).

Exam tip ✔ 72

- Don't try to guess the answer from your own knowledge. Always find the answer in the text.

		A: YES	B: NO
1	Experts believe that objects will have a very different appearance in the future.	☐	☐
2	In the house of the future the heating will come on after a single instruction.	☐	☐
3	The pictures on the walls might change as people go in and out of rooms.	☐	☐
4	One simple action will be enough to prepare the living room for watching a film.	☐	☐
5	It might be possible to use furniture to display photographs.	☐	☐
6	The fridge will inform the home-owner when it's time to replace a broken part.	☐	☐
7	The fridge will suggest recipes based on what ingredients are inside it.	☐	☐
8	The computer chips needed to make the system work are cheap.	☐	☐
9	The chip in your shirt will tell you when the shirt needs to be washed.	☐	☐
10	The bedroom mirror will tell you if the clothes you are wearing suit you.	☐	☐

The House of the Future

The future is coming, but, according to the experts, it probably won't look like the set of a science fiction film. Everyday items will look pretty much like those we see around us today. But under the surface, things are changing, and in twenty years' time the products we use will definitely be able to do a lot more than they can today.

One place where we are likely to see big changes is in the home. Developments in hardware and software will make everyday living simple and easy. When you walk into a room, the lights and heating will come on automatically and your favourite music will start to play without you having to do or say anything. It may even be possible to program the system to display artwork that suits individual family members' personal tastes as they go around the house.

In the living room, pressing a single button on the remote control will lower the lights, close the curtains, and switch off the music as the system realises that a movie is about to start. New touch-screen technology built into the furniture means that the dining room table could become a computer screen. You might be able to place a mobile phone on a table and see digital pictures in its glass surface that were taken with the phone at school or work.

In the kitchen, the refrigerator could be connected to the internet. It would 'talk' to the supplier, and order replacement parts without you ever knowing something was wrong. This fridge will be able to tell you what's inside it, making the job of creating a shopping list much easier. And, as you remove the food from the fridge, and place it on the counter top, another computer there will recognise what it is and begin to suggest recipes.

This is all possible because tiny, inexpensive computer chips will be attached to every product in the house, including your clothes. So, the washing machine will know how to wash your favourite linen shirt and your wardrobe will be able to tell you which clothes are at the dry-cleaner's and when they are due back. An interactive mirror in the bedroom may allow you to see how you look in different clothes without the need to try them on.

Unfortunately, one thing we are unlikely to see in the next few years is a human-like household robot. We will have to wait a bit longer for that!

5 Which of the ideas in the article will most improve our lives and which are a waste of time? Why? Can you think of any other things that would make your life easier?

(109) Language focus: predicting the future

6 Complete the sentences according to what is said in the article, using the words and phrases in the box.

> could likely may might ~~probably won't~~ unlikely will definitely

0 The future _probably won't_ look like the set of a science fiction film.
1 The products of the future _____ be better than today's.
2 We are _____ to see big changes in the home.
3 The dining room table _____ become a computer screen.
4 We _____ be able to see photographs in a table top.
5 An interactive mirror _____ let you see yourself in different clothes.
6 It is _____ that human-like household robots will be available.

7 Choose the correct words to complete these rules.

1 *Will*, *could*, *may* and *might* are followed by infinitive **with / without** *to*.
2 *Likely* and *unlikely* are used with the verb *to be* in the **future / present**.
3 Adverbs like *probably* and *definitely* go **before / after** *will* and **before / after** *won't*.

Speaking

8 Work in groups to make predictions about these things.

> clothes entertainment food transport health space travel

9 Present your ideas from Activity 8 to the rest of the class. Which group's ideas do you think are most likely to come true?

> In the future, cars will probably use less petrol than they do now.

Unless we act now ...

E Listening Part 3 • Speaking Part 2 | **V** weather | **L** first conditional and *unless*

Vocabulary: weather

1 Which words can go with which pictures?

a lack of rain __   a storm __   drought __   floods __   heavy rain __
high temperatures __   hot summers __   ice __   lightning __
low temperatures __   mild winters __   snow __   thunder __   wildfires __

2 What kind of weather do these places have?

Australia   Canada   Great Britain   Greenland   Mexico   Thailand

3 Describe the climate where you live. Have you noticed any changes in the weather over the past few years?

Exam practice: Listening Part 3

 Exam tip ✔90

- Use the time before the listening starts to read the question paper.
- Easy words like days and months must be spelt correctly.

4 You will hear a radio presenter giving some information about an exhibition on global warming. For each question, fill in the missing information in the numbered space.

> ### New exhibition on global warming at the Science Museum – A Changing World
>
> The exhibition begins on **(1)** _____
>
> The exhibition floor is covered with **(2)** _____
>
> Display about the Arctic includes - a large block of ice
>
>   - several **(3)** _____
>
> The exhibition posters were written by famous **(4)** _____
>
> Short films – stories from people living in Australia, Brazil, Greenland and **(5)** _____
>
> At the end of the exhibition you can send a message to a politician or a **(6)** _____

5 Do you think this exhibition will make people change their behaviour?

Reading

6 Work with a partner. Complete the article with these numbers.

2   30%   10   650,000   1990   5   30

Temperatures are rising around the world, particularly in the Arctic. In the past **(1)**_____ years, **(2)**_____ square kilometres of ice have disappeared. Rising sea levels mean that many countries are going to lose part of their coastline. Unless we take action, some countries will completely disappear. Scientists think that if temperatures continue to increase, we will see hotter summers, milder winters and more tropical storms, which might become more dangerous. They also say that if global temperatures rise by just **(3)**_____ degrees, **(4)**_____ of all land-living creatures may become extinct.

The **(5)**_____ hottest years ever recorded have all been since **(6)**_____ . Scientists say that unless we reduce the amount of pollution we are creating, temperatures could be **(7)**_____ degrees higher by the end of the century.

If we take action now, we can make a big difference. What are you going to do?

Language booster

going to

We use *going to* when we can see evidence of what is going to happen.
Rising sea levels mean that many countries are going to lose part of their coastline.
We also use *going to* to ask and talk about plans and intentions.
What are you going to do?

---

109 **Language focus:** first conditional and *unless*

7 Underline five conditional sentences in the text above. Then choose the correct words to complete the rules.

1 In first conditional sentences, the *if* clause is in **present simple / future 'will'**.
2 The modal verb **will / may / might / can / could** can't be used in the main clause.
3 *Unless* means **if ... not / when**.

8 Complete the leaflet about ways to help the environment. Fill each space with *if* or *unless*.

How can I help?

There are lots of ways you can help cut pollution and prevent global warming. They are simple things, but **(0)**____*if*____ we all do them, they can make a big difference.

• Don't turn the heating on **(1)**_____ you really need it.
• **(2)**_____ you are choosing between two different products, choose the one with the least packaging.
• Switch off the TV and DVD player **(3)**_____ someone is using them.
• **(4)**_____ you go to school by car, take a friend with you.
• Use the microwave instead of the cooker **(5)**_____ you want to heat something small.
• **(6)**_____ your clothes are very dirty, wash them in cold water.

9 Which of the things in the leaflet do you already do? Which are you going to do in the future?

Exam tip ✔96

• Don't worry if you don't agree with your partner. Give your own opinion and explain why you disagree.

Exam practice: Speaking Part 2

10 Work in pairs. Look at the picture on page 63. Your friend wants to help the environment. Talk together about the things he can do, and decide which are the most important.

Review 3

1 Which word is the odd one out in each group, and why?

0 (novelist) pianist violinist guitarist
'novelist' because the others are all musicians
1 proud disappointed nervous jealous
2 helmet trainers gloves goal
3 snow rain thunder ice
4 Geography Biology Maths university

5 track racket pitch court
6 certificate homework essay project
7 chip program network digital
8 classroom timetable corridor laboratory
9 storm mild hot heavy
10 scientist journalist student chef

2 Make predictions about the year 2100 using the prompts given. Change word forms where necessary.

0 We / probably / able / travel / quick / than today.
We will probably be able to travel more quickly than today.
1 Robots / able / do housework / well / than today.
2 Cars / go / far / on / one litre of petrol / than today.
3 We / able / heat houses / cheap / than today.
4 We / likely / use / cash / less / than today.
5 We / probably / not live / healthy / than today.

3 In pairs, say whether you agree or disagree with the predictions in Activity 2.

4 Read the information about the competition and complete the sentences with the words in the box.

can doesn't have to ~~have to~~ if must unless

Photography Competition – 'My Environment'

- **The competition is open to students aged 16–21.**
- **The deadline is 31 October.**
- **Up to three photos allowed per person.**
- **Send a short title or explanation (maximum 60 words) with each picture.**
- **No photos will be accepted without the official entry form.**
- **Photos can be in black and white or colour.**

0 'You *have to* be between 16 and 21 years of age to enter.'
1 '............. your photo arrives after 31 October it won't be included in the competition.'
2 'Each person .... send in up to three photos.'
3 You .... include a short explanation with each picture.'
4 'Your photo won't be accepted .... you use the official entry form.'
5 'Your photo .... be in colour, it can be in black and white.'

5 Complete this text by choosing the correct pronoun.

I want to be a paediatrician – a doctor (0) **who / whose** cares for children. This has been my dream since I was little. It all started (1) **where / when** I had a babysitter (2) **which / who** wanted to be a doctor. She got me interested in medicine. I've worked hard towards my goal. My Biology teacher, (3) **whose / which** father is a doctor, has always encouraged me. This year she arranged for me to take a special class (4) **where / which** you choose something (5) **who / that** you are interested in and do a project on it. I worked in a hospital for three weeks, (6) **when / where** I saw for myself exactly what a paediatrician does. Now I am more determined than ever to become a doctor.

6 Make questions in the present perfect using one of the words in the box.

argue fail have lose meet travel ~~win~~

0 *Have you ever won* a competition?
1 _____ a famous person?
2 _____ in a plane?
3 _____ a mobile phone?
4 _____ with a friend?
5 _____ an exam?
6 _____ a job interview?

7 Ask a partner the questions in Activity 6, and write sentences about them. If your partner answers *yes* to any questions, ask for details.

Samantha has never met a famous person, but she has travelled by plane. She went to Florida on holiday last year.

8 Choose the best option to complete the sentences.

0 I think I'll get the job *if /* **unless** I say something silly in the job interview.
1 I'll be really disappointed if I **don't / won't** get the job.
2 **If / Unless** I feel anxious, I might ask my best friend to help me calm down.
3 **If / Unless** I am confident in the interview, I won't get the job.
4 My mum **is / will be** proud of me if I get the job.
5 I'll be amazed **if / unless** I don't get the job!
6 If I want to own my own business one day, I **have to / will have to** work really hard.

On target?

How well can you do these things?	☆	☆☆	☆☆☆
E read for detailed understanding			
E listen and complete someone's notes			
E communicate information in a written message			
E read for the main message			
V talk about sports and competitions			
V talk about education and work			
V talk about computers and technology			
L use comparative and superlative adverbs			
L use present perfect for general experience and recent past			
L talk about obligation, prohibition and permission			
L talk about future probability and use first conditional			

E **Exam skills**   V **Vocabulary skills**   L **Language skills**

10.1 If I visited your country...

E Listening Part 4 · Reading Part 4 | V holidays | L second conditional

Vocabulary: holidays

1 Match the reasons that people go on holiday to the pictures.

to do something challenging __	to enjoy beautiful scenery __
to learn about new places __	to learn a new skill __
to look at famous buildings __	to relax __

Exam tip ✔92

- If you don't know the answer to a question, make a guess because it might be correct.
- Never leave a blank on your answer sheet.

Exam practice: Listening Part 4

🔊 17 **2** You will hear a conversation between a woman, Shona, and her husband, Jim, about where to go on holiday. Decide if each sentence is correct (A) or incorrect (B).

	A: YES	B: NO
1 Shona would like to have the same holiday as the previous year.	☐	☐
2 Shona thinks there would be problems if they went on the cruise.	☐	☐
3 Jim and Shona would both enjoy a week relaxing on a beach.	☐	☐
4 Jim suggests learning a new skill on holiday.	☐	☐
5 Shona persuades Jim to do a diving course with her.	☐	☐
6 Shona and Jim decide to go to a travel agent to book.	☐	☐

🔍110 ## Language focus: second conditional

3 Match the sentence halves from the conversation.

1 Would we enjoy it as much   A if we spent a week lying on the beach.
2 If it rained all the time,   B we could explore underwater.
3 We'd be bored   C we wouldn't see the scenery.
4 If we learned to dive,   D if we went there again?

Language booster

If I were you ...

We often use *if I were you,* to give advice.
If I were you, I'd book a hotel on the internet.

4 Choose the correct words to complete the rules.

1 We use second conditional for situations which are **real / imagined**.
2 The *if* clause **always comes first / can come first or second**.
3 We use *would* in the *if* / **main** clause.
4 We can use *could* or *might* instead of *would* in the *if* / **main** clause.

5 Complete the questions using second conditional.

0 If you could go anywhere for a holiday, where _would you go_ (you / go)?
1 If you _____ (win) a holiday for two people, who would you invite?
2 If you _____ (can learn) a new skill on holiday, what would it be?
3 _____ (you / be bored) if you went on a cruise?

6 With a partner, ask and answer the questions above. Do you have similar ideas about holidays?

Exam practice: Reading Part 4

7 Read the text and questions below. For each question, circle the correct letter A, B, C or D.

Travelling abroad

by Josh Simms

Why do tourists think that the first thing they should do when they visit a new place is go and see cathedrals, museums and monuments? There are many things I like about travelling, but queuing up to buy museum tickets then having your visit ruined by noisy tour groups is not one of them. The things that make places special are all around the famous buildings, not inside them.

My recent trip to India is a good example of this. By far the most interesting part of it was getting to know people – bicycle-taxi drivers, policemen riding elephants and children trying to earn some money by cleaning shoes. It was all so amazing that I didn't need to do any 'proper' sightseeing.

I also have fantastic memories of Florence. It was a boiling hot day and the queue to the art gallery was at least a kilometre long. Instead of joining it I sat in a shady square, ate a delicious pizza and listened to a man singing opera songs to only a few listeners. If I had stuck to my original plan I would have missed this experience.

One of the best things about travelling is creating memories to bring back. When I got back home from a holiday in Malaysia, I made some of the dishes I'd tasted in the food market. Maybe my results weren't as good as the real thing, but they reminded me of the places and the people I'd met – far better than anything from a souvenir shop.

1 What is Josh trying to do in this article?
A explain what he likes to do on holiday
B recommend places for tourists to visit
C complain about the way tourists behave
D describe his favourite holiday destination

2 In India, Josh enjoyed
A going round famous buildings.
B riding on an elephant.
C talking to different people.
D playing with children.

3 On his trip to Florence, Josh
A got away from the crowds.
B went to the opera.
C visited the art gallery.
D walked around in the sunshine.

4 The Malaysian food that Josh made at home
A was difficult to prepare.
B was better than the market food.
C didn't taste very good.
D brought back happy memories.

5 Which postcard would Josh write to his friend?

A
I went round this museum of local history with a group and the guide gave us lots of interesting information.

C
I've done the cathedral, the castle and the art gallery and I'm looking forward to the museum.

B
I haven't visited any of the important sights but I've learnt a lot about this interesting country.

D
This is a fantastic place – lots of souvenir shops with very reasonable prices.

Speaking

8 If Josh Simms came to your country, what would he enjoy doing? Plan a weekend holiday in your country for Josh. Think about these things:

Where could he go?   What would you show him?
How would he travel?   Where could he stay?

CDs can be bought online

E Reading Part 2 | V music and festivals | L modal passives

Exam practice: Reading Part 2

1 The people below all want to go to a music festival. Underneath, there are eight descriptions of music festivals. Decide which festival would be the most suitable for the following people.

1 Tom and Rosa want to camp at a big event. They plan to stay up all night to see as many different kinds of bands as possible.

2 Luis and Jorge want to spend a day at a festival in an attractive location. They want to attend some other cultural activities as well as listen to music.

3 Rachel and Cecy want to camp at a festival to celebrate the end of the college year. They want to hear their favourite bands and enjoy fun activities with people their own age.

4 Students Matt, Mel, Sam and Ollie play traditional music in their own band. As well as hearing some great sounds, they want to improve their playing and hope to get a chance to perform.

5 Paul and Helen and their 11-year-old twins want to camp at a small festival where there will be plenty of entertainment for them all. They can't spend much money.

The best of this summer's Music Festivals

A Upbeat
With 75,000 visitors expected and 100 of the best bands from both sides of the Atlantic, Upbeat is the original and biggest hard-rock festival with three days of non-stop music from 10 a.m. to midnight. Camping and day tickets are still available.

B Barnsby
Several stars of the current folk scene are booked for this small informal festival. There will be teaching sessions for players, who can then display their skills at a late night stage show. Kids under eleven go free and can enjoy fun educational activities. No tents but discounts for festival goers at local guesthouses.

C Beat Village
This festival attracts over 20,000 party-goers of all ages, with a 24-hour line-up of bands for every musical taste. There is also a huge range of stalls selling food, clothing and items from around the world. You'll have to hurry though – the last few camping places are selling fast!

D Longitude
You'll hear many kinds of music plus stand-up comedy, poetry readings and music workshops at this unusual festival. The beautiful site is set among rolling hills. There are 15,000 free camping places, and no entry charge for children under seven. Twelve-hour tickets are available to non-campers.

E Global gathering
The world's biggest electronic music weekend takes place on a former airfield and offers performance spots for new bands. Only day tickets are left now but hotel accommodation is available nearby. The event is for over 18s only.

F Beachball
If you have just finished your exams, head down to the golden sands for this student-only festival. The most popular bands of the year will be there, plus surfing, crazy sports and a fancy dress competition. The three-day ticket includes camping on the beach.

G Animal magic
60,000 visitors are expected at this most unusual festival venue – a zoo. There will be mainstream bands plus indie, hiphop and drum n'bass sounds until midnight each day. There are discounts for kids under sixteen at the zoo and nearby funfair. Tickets are still available.

H Oak Tree
This festival is limited to 5,000 campers, with no day tickets. The line-up includes music, poetry, theatre, and comedy. Children under twelve go free, with activities such as puppet shows and drumming lessons provided for them. The friendly atmosphere continues into the evening with singing round the campfire.

Vocabulary: music and festivals

2 Find the following in texts A–H in Activity 1:

1 four kinds of music
2 three places to stay overnight
3 four kinds of entertainments for children
4 four kinds of non-musical entertainments for adults

Speaking

3 You and your partner want to go to a festival. Talk together about the festivals in Activity 1 and decide which you will go to.

110 ## Language focus: modal passives

4 Match the festival information to the explanations.

1 You can find cash machines by the main stage.

2 You should wear your festival wristband at all times.

3 You mustn't bring glass bottles onto the festival site.

Essential information for festival visitors

A Your festival wristband should be worn at all times.
B Cash machines can be found by the main stage.
C Glass bottles must not be brought onto the festival site.

5 Choose the correct words to complete the rules.

1 We form the modal passive with a modal verb + *be* + **infinitive** / **past participle**.
2 We often use the modal passive for **official notices** / **talking to friends**.

6 Write these festival rules.

0 Lockers / can / rent / for storing valuable items.
Lockers can be rented for storing valuable items.
1 Toilets and washrooms / must / leave / clean after use.
2 Mobile phones / can / re-charge / at the festival office.
3 Pets / should / not bring / to the festival.
4 All belongings / must / remove / on leaving the campsite.

Writing

7 Work in groups to design your own festival. Think about these things:

Where will it be?   What kind of music will you have?
How long will it be?   What festival rules will you have?

8 Write a paragraph about your festival.

9 Read about all of the festivals your class has designed. Decide which one you would most like to go to. Whose festival will be the busiest?

11.1 My great new leather jacket

E Listening Part 1 • Writing Part 1 | **V** clothes | **L** adjective order

Vocabulary: clothes

1 Match the words to the things in the pictures.

belt __ boots __ coat __ dress __ handbag __
high heels __ jeans __ skirt __ sweater / jumper __
top __ T-shirt __ trousers __

2 Which of the two places would you prefer to shop in? Why?

Exam tip ✔85

• You will hear each dialogue twice. Use the second listening to check, and to answer any questions you missed the first time.

Exam practice: Listening Part 1

3 For each question there are three pictures and a short recording. Choose the correct picture and put a tick (✓) in the box below it.

1 Which shop do they decide to meet in later?

 A ☐    B ☐    C ☐

2 On which floor can you get a free gift?

 A ☐    B ☐    C ☐

3 What did Donna buy yesterday?

 A ☐    B ☐    C ☐

4 How will Danny buy the computer game?

 A ☐    B ☐   C ☐

Language focus: adjective order

4 Look at the example and write the categories of adjective in the correct order.

*Buy one of our **exciting new stripy woollen** jumpers.*

| colour / pattern | material | opinion | size / age / shape |

opinion → ☐ → ☐ → ☐

5 Use the words in the box to describe the clothes in the pictures.

blue bright brown cotton denim leather orange pale patterned
plastic pretty red short silk sporty trendy ugly white

In the first picture, there's a sporty pale blue cotton T-shirt.

Exam practice: Writing Part 1

6 Here are some sentences about shopping habits. For each question, complete the second sentence so that it means the same as the first. Use no more than three words.

0 Boys' shopping habits are just like girls'.
Boys have _the same_ shopping habits as girls.

1 Boys usually buy cheaper clothes than girls.
Girls usually buy _____ clothes than boys.

2 Boys only go shopping if they need a particular item.
Boys don't go shopping _____ need a particular item.

3 Boys often look on the internet before they spend their money.
Boys often don't spend their money until _____ on the internet.

4 Shopping with friends is girls' favourite social activity.
Shopping with friends is the social activity _____ the most.

Reading

7 Do you think the sentences in Activity 6 are true or false?

0 _F_   1 ___   2 ___   3 ___   4 ___

8 Read this article and check your answers.

REVEALED: **Teen shopping trends!**

Girls spend more time shopping and buy more, according to **YOU!** Our **TEEN! survey** asked over a thousand young people about their shopping habits.

The results showed that:

☺ boys tend to save their money for one expensive item, such as a pair of designer jeans or trainers. Girls, on the other hand, buy several cheaper items, which they can mix and match with their other clothes.

☺ boys often check out the thing they want to buy in magazines or on the internet, and only go to a shop once they have decided exactly what they want. For most girls, however, shopping is very enjoyable. Many girls said that their favourite activity was a weekly shopping trip with their friends, even if they didn't buy anything.

What do **YOU** think? Email your comments to shopping@TEEN.mag.uk.

Speaking

9 Look at the article again and write the questions that the researchers asked. Ask and answer them with a partner.

Do you buy clothes with designer labels?

No, I don't. I prefer...

Exam practice: Reading Part 1

1 Look at the photos and discuss the questions.

    1 What are these places?   2 Why would you go to each one?

2 Match the notices to four of the places above.

A Clothes left in these changing rooms will be thrown away after three months.

B Please take your vegetables to be weighed at the checkout.

C Socks must be worn with hired bowling shoes.

D Free gift wrapping service on any item of £10 or more.

3 Look at the text in each notice. What does it say? Circle the correct letter A, B or C.

1   A   We will not keep any clothes here for longer than three months.
       B   You can collect clothes from the changing rooms after three months.
       C   Clothes thrown away here can be collected in three months' time.
2   A   You can weigh your fruit yourself at the checkout.
       B   The checkout assistant will weigh your fruit for you.
       C   When you have weighed your fruit take it to the checkout.
3   A   You cannot wear the bowling alley's shoes if you don't have socks on.
       B   If you want to bowl, you have to hire socks.
       C   It is not essential to hire bowling shoes unless you wear socks.
4   A   It costs £10 to use our gift wrapping service.
       B   If you spend £10 on a gift there is no charge for wrapping it.
       C   You get a free gift worth £10 if you have your gift wrapped at the shop.

Vocabulary: money

4 Complete the sentences with the words in the box. Do you agree?

> cash   credit card   discount   receipt   tip

1 I never throw away a _____ in case I have to take something back to the shop.
2 I think that students should get a _____ in every shop because they don't have enough money to pay full price.
3 It's important to leave a _____ of at least 12% in a restaurant.
4 I don't like using a _____ because it's easy to spend more than you can afford. I'd rather pay by _____.

Exam tip ✔68

- Some options will look similar to the notice, and may use the same words.
- Read all three options slowly and carefully before you choose.

🔍 111 Language focus: *have / get something done*

5 Look at the list. Write *M* next to the things you do yourself. Write *S* by the ones that somebody else does for you.

1 brush your hair ____
2 cut your hair ____
3 check your teeth ____
4 clean your teeth ____
5 mend your clothes ____
6 do your homework ____
7 fix your bicycle ____
8 test your eyes ____

6 To talk about a job that somebody else does for us, we use:

have / get + noun + past participle.

Make sentences about the things from Activity 5 that someone else does for you.

I have my hair cut by the hairdresser.

Exam tip ✔90

- Before listening, think about what kinds of words the answers will be.
- You will hear the exact words you need, you don't have to change them.

🔊 19

Exam practice: Listening Part 3

7 You will hear a tour guide talking to a group of young people about a trip to a shopping centre. Listen and circle the places that she mentions.

art studios   bank   beauty salon   cinema   dry cleaner's
information desk   internet café   pet shop   post office   restaurant

8 Listen again. For each question, fill in the missing information in the numbered space.

Golden Court Shopping Centre
Leaving time: (0) ___4___ p.m.
Money: change foreign money on the (1) _____ floor
Cinema: check film ends before (2) _____ p.m.
Painting: where: near the main entrance
            cost: around (3) £_____ ; time: 1½ hours
Phones: use the special service in the (4) _____
Lunch: show Travel Tours badge to get a (5) _____
            from Pronto Pizzas
Problems: go to the (6) _____

Speaking

9 Work with a partner to plan a new shopping centre. What unusual facilities will you include to make your shopping centre different?

12.1 I'd never seen a film before

E Speaking Parts 3 & 4 • Writing Part 3 (story) | V cinema | L past perfect

Vocabulary: cinema

1 Put the words below into one of three categories:

A Describing a film   B At the cinema   C Types of film

action ___	fantasy ___	science fiction ___
adventure ___	historical drama ___	screen ___
advertisement ___	musical ___	seat ___
animation ___	performance ___	special effects ___
audience ___	popcorn ___	star ___
character ___	romance ___	thriller ___
comedy ___	row ___	ticket ___
curtain ___	scene ___	

Exam practice: Speaking Parts 3 and 4

2 You are each going to describe a photograph that shows someone watching a film. Work in pairs, taking it in turns to be the examiner and the student. Student A: describe photograph 1. Student B: describe photograph 2.

3 Your photos both showed people watching films. Talk together about the different kinds of films you like watching, and say where and when you like to watch them.

Listening

4 Discuss the questions with your partner.

1 What can you remember about the first time you went to the cinema?
2 How much TV did you watch before you were five?
3 What did you enjoy about going to the cinema when you were little?
4 How are films different now from how they were when you were five?
5 What was the name of the first film you ever saw in the cinema?

 5 Listen to a retired film director talking about his first visit to a cinema. How would he answer the questions in Activity 4?

112 **Language focus:** past perfect

6 Read the example and write *yes* or *no* beside the sentences below. If you wrote *no*, correct the sentence.

*My father **felt** guilty because he **had left** me with a babysitter the night before.*

1 The actions in this sentence happened at different times in the past. ____
2 The first verb is in past perfect. The second is in past simple. ____
3 We use past perfect for the action which happened first. ____
4 We form past perfect with *had* + infinitive. ____
5 We often use past perfect when we are telling a story. ____

7 Read the story. Put the verbs in brackets into past simple or past perfect.

A strange coincidence

One evening when I was about 16, my younger sister Daniela and I (1)_____ (decide) to go to the cinema. We wanted to see *Grease*, with John Travolta and Olivia Newton John. It was an incredibly popular film at that time and we were the only people in our school who (2)_____ (not see) it.
About an hour after the film had started, the fire alarm (3)_____ (go off) and we all had to leave the cinema. I got separated from my sister. Of course mobile phones (4)_____ (not exist) then so I couldn't just call her and ask her where she was. When I (5)_____ (get) home, the first thing my Dad said was "Where's Daniela?" I (6)_____ (never see) my father get angry before, but that time he did.
A short time later, my sister arrived home. She (7)_____ (catch) the wrong bus and had got terribly lost. Luckily she had met a kind lady who (8)_____ (bring) her home.
Several years later we were invited to a wedding. The bride was a friend of my sister's and when we were introduced to her aunt, we (9)_____ (recognise) her as the lady who (10)_____ (help) my sister all those years before!

Exam practice: Writing Part 3 (story)

8 Read the exam task.

> • Your English teacher has asked you to write a story.
> • Your story must begin with this sentence:
>
>   *Just as the film began, I received a text message on my mobile phone.*
>
> • Write your story in about 100 words.

Plan your story with a partner. Think about these questions:

1 Who were you with?
2 What kind of film were you going to see?
3 Who sent you the message?
4 What had happened?
5 What did you do?

9 Write your story. When you have finished, read the checklist on page 63 and make changes if you need to.

10 Work with a partner. Read each other's stories. Say two positive things and make one suggestion for improvement.

12.2 My agent asked me to work

E Reading Part 4 | **V** reporting verbs | **L** reported speech

They said it would be fun!

So, you think you'd like to be a film extra? Well, read this description of Chris Maitland's last job and then decide!

When my phone rang last Thursday, I recognised the number immediately as my agent Caroline's. She asked if I wanted to work the next day on a film called *Day of Disaster*. My diary was full that week, but I said I would cancel my plans for the next day. I was worried that if I turned her down now, she would never offer me work again. Also, I needed the money.

I arrived at the film set on time, at 5 a.m., still half asleep. The assistant director told me to go to the costume department, where they put lots of nasty, sticky make-up on me to make it look like I had been in an accident. Then, for the next few hours, we just had to wait.

Most of us had forgotten to bring anything to read and we were too far away to watch the filming, so we passed the morning talking and joking together. Finally, the assistant director came over. He told me I was going to play a blind man and put a bandage over my eyes. During the filming, the other extras had to look after me. Some time after lunch, I took off my bandage and threw it away. The assistant director asked me what I had done with it, but I told him I'd accidentally lost it that afternoon. Luckily he believed me!

At 7 p.m., the director said we could go and have our make-up removed. I was so keen to get home I got straight into my car still covered in blood and dirt. I don't know what the garage staff thought when I stopped to fill up with petrol!

Exam practice: Reading Part 4

1 **Read the article and questions. For each question, circle the correct letter A, B, C or D.**

1 What is the writer doing in the text?
 A giving advice on how to become a film extra
 B explaining why he wanted to become a film extra
 C giving an accurate description of the work of film extras
 D complaining about the conditions in which film extras work

2 What does Chris say about Caroline's offer of work?
 A He felt he had to accept it, even though he had something else to do.
 B He was a bit disappointed with the kind of work she offered.
 C He was excited because he thought the film sounded interesting.
 D He was surprised at the amount of money she offered.

3 Chris spent his time in the waiting area
 A chatting to the other extras.
 B putting his make-up and costume on.
 C reading the book he had brought with him.
 D watching the stars of the film performing.

4 Why did the other extras have to help Chris?
 A He got injured during filming.
 B He couldn't see what he was doing.
 C He had never done this kind of work before.
 D He had thrown away part of his costume.

5 What would Chris say about his day as a film extra?

A *I felt lively at the beginning of the day, but by the end I was really tired and couldn't wait to get home.*

B *I was held up in traffic in the morning but once I got there I enjoyed getting dressed up in my costume.*

C *Most of the people there were very friendly but I didn't get on with the assistant director – I had an argument with him.*

D *It was a long day, although we didn't do that much work. We finished late so I didn't stay behind to get cleaned up.*

Exam tip ✔ 74

- Read all the options carefully and think about the meaning. Don't choose an option just because it contains a word or idea from the text.

🔍 112 **Language focus:** reported speech

2 Look at the examples from the text and choose the correct words to complete the rules.

'I'll cancel my plans for tomorrow.'
➜ *I said I would cancel my plans for the next day.*
'You're going to play a blind man.'
➜ *He told me I was going to play a blind man.*
'I accidentally lost it this afternoon.'
➜ *I told him I had accidentally lost it that afternoon.*
'You can go and have your make-up removed.'
➜ *The director said we could go and have our make-up removed.*

1   In reported speech the tense usually moves **back / forward**.
2   Time expressions like *tomorrow* usually **change / stay the same**.
3   Both *say* and *tell* are used in reported speech. **Say / Tell** needs an object (*me, him, her,* etc).

3 Write what the person actually said, or report what they said.

0   I told my friends I couldn't go out with them the next day.
I said, '___*I can't*___ go out with you _*tomorrow*_.'
1   I asked my agent how much I would get paid.
I asked my agent, 'How much _____ get paid?'
2   I said, 'What _____ me to do?'
I asked the director what he wanted me to do.
3   The director said we had to pretend to be in pain.
The director said, 'You _____ pretend to be in pain.'
4   I said, 'I am too tired to get my make-up removed.'
I told him _____ too tired to get my make-up removed.

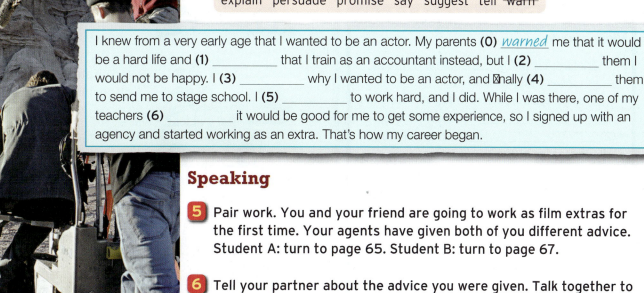

Vocabulary: reporting verbs

4 Complete the text with the correct form of the verbs below. There may be more than one right answer.

explain   persuade   promise   say   suggest   tell   ~~warn~~

I knew from a very early age that I wanted to be an actor. My parents **(0)** _*warned*_ me that it would be a hard life and **(1)** _____ that I train as an accountant instead, but I **(2)** _____ them I would not be happy. I **(3)** _____ why I wanted to be an actor, and finally **(4)** _____ them to send me to stage school. I **(5)** _____ to work hard, and I did. While I was there, one of my teachers **(6)** _____ it would be good for me to get some experience, so I signed up with an agency and started working as an extra. That's how my career began.

Speaking

5 Pair work. You and your friend are going to work as film extras for the first time. Your agents have given both of you different advice. Student A: turn to page 65. Student B: turn to page 67.

6 Tell your partner about the advice you were given. Talk together to decide which pieces of advice were good and which were bad. When you have decided, turn to page 63 to check.

1 Which adjectives can go with which nouns?

actor	film	handbag	souvenirs
	action-packed		

~~action-packed~~ cheap
cultural documentary
fashionable handsome
interesting leather
plastic red short
talented ugly young

2 Complete each sentence with a noun and three adjectives from Activity 1.

1 Before the main movie, we watched an

_____.

2 Colin Attwell is a _____

_____ with a huge fan club.

3 That _____

costs more than most people earn in a week.

4 I didn't bring anything back from my holiday because the shops only sold _____

_____.

3 Complete the store visitor guide with these words and phrases, and put the words in brackets into passive voice.

Backpacks   doorways and fire escapes
Eating and drinking   Large items   photos
~~Motorcycle helmets~~   staff and managers

Harrods Department Store
Visitor guide

- **(0)** *Motorcycle helmets should be removed*
  (should remove) when entering the store.
- To prevent damage to displays or injuries to other customers,
  (1)_____ (should carry) by hand.
- **(2)**_____ (can hand in) at the
  Left Luggage office by Door 3.
- **(3)**_____ (permit) in the
  restaurant areas only.
- For security reasons **(4)**_____ (may not take) in the jewellery or antique furniture departments.
- All **(5)**_____ (should keep) clear.

The **(6)**_____
of Harrods Department Store wish you
a pleasant visit.

4 Look at the pictures and prompts, and write sentences in second conditional.

0 [win lottery / buy boat]
*If I won the lottery,
I'd buy a boat.*
_____

1 [buy boat / sail to
South Africa]
_____
_____
_____

2 [sail to South Africa /
go on safari]
_____
_____
_____

3 [go on safari / see
elephants and giraffes]
_____
_____
_____

4 [see elephants and
giraffes / take lots of
photos]
_____
_____
_____

5 Read the pairs of sentences and underline the one that happened first. Join the sentences using the conjunction in brackets and past simple or past perfect.

0 Holly was very excited. <u>She won tickets to the festival.</u> (because)
Holly was very excited because she'd won tickets to the festival.

1 Her friends Rachel and Jess went the year before. They told her what to take. (so)

2 She left the tent poles at home. Holly tried to put her tent up. (but)

3 Luckily there was space in her friends' tent. Holly remembered to bring her sleeping bag. (and)

4 They unpacked their bags. They went to explore the festival. (after)

5 They reached the main stage. The band already started playing and they missed the first two songs. (by the time)

6 They finally went to bed. They saw lots of different acts and spent some time in the dance tent. (when)

6 Read the newspaper article about fashion designer Evan Rapier and complete the conversation.

Evan Rapier told me that he'd loved clothes ever since he was a child, and had designed his first collection of clothes at the age of 15. I asked why he mixed so many patterns and bright colours together and he replied that he believed that fashion should be fun. He suggested I come to his show, which was going to be very exciting. He even offered me a free ticket. Unfortunately I couldn't go that evening but I promised that I wouldn't miss his next show.

REPORTER: How long **(0)** *have you been* (you be) interested in clothes?

EVAN: I **(1)**_____ (love) clothes, ever since I **(2)**_____ (be) a child. I **(3)**_____ (design) my first collection of clothes at the age of fifteen.

REPORTER: Why **(4)**_____ (you mix) so many patterns and bright colours together?

EVAN: I **(5)**_____ (believe) fashion should be fun. How about **(6)**_____ (come) to my show? It **(7)**_____ (be) very exciting. **(8)**_____ (you like) a free ticket?'

REPORTER: Unfortunately I **(9)**_____ (can not) come this evening. I **(10)**_____ (not miss) your next one.

7 What can you have done in these places?

beautician's   optician's   doctor's   dentist's

You can have your nails painted at the beautician's.

On target?

How well can you do these things?	☆	☆☆	☆☆☆
E listen for detailed meaning and speaker opinion			
E read for key information and writer opinion			
E rephrase information using different set structures			
E describe a photograph and manage a conversation			
V talk about holidays, festivals and films			
V talk about clothes, money and services			
L use the second conditional			
L recognise and understand the modal passive			
L use the past perfect to tell a story			
L understand and use reported speech			

E **Exam skills**   V **Vocabulary skills**   L **Language skills**

Pairwork activities

Unit 3 Lesson 1: Student A

Unit 3 Lesson 1: Student B

Unit 9 Lesson 2

10 Your friend wants to help the environment. Talk together about the things he can do, and decide which are the most important.

Unit 12 Lesson 1

9 Writing Part 3 checklist

The story has about 100 words. ☐
There is a beginning, a middle and an end. ☐
The story leads on logically from the opening sentence. ☐
There are two or three paragraphs. ☐
The story happens in the past. ☐
A variety of tenses are used. ☐
Capital letters and other punctuation are used correctly. ☐
Sentences start with a variety of different words. ☐
Conjunctions such as *after that* and *finally* are used correctly. ☐
There are no spelling mistakes. ☐

Unit 12 Lesson 2

6

Rules for Film Extras

1 Never arrive late.
2 Don't speak to the stars.
3 Take a book or crossword with you.
4 Don't bring friends or pets with you.
5 Ask what kind of clothes you should wear.
6 Don't bring a camera.
7 Fill in your form and hand it in at the end of the day.

Unit 3 Lesson 2: Student A

7 Ask your partner questions to complete the sentences.

1 The Romans built a city where London now stands. They called it _____ (What?).
   What did the Romans call London?
2 The Tower of London was built in the _____ (When?) by King William.
3 In the 15th century, houses in London were made of _____ (What?).
4 In the 16th century, ships were sent from London to _____ (Why?).
5 A theatre called The Globe was built in London during this time. Plays by _____ (Who?) were performed here.
6 In 1666, a fire started _____ (Where?). 80% of the city of London was destroyed.
7 Queen Victoria ruled from 1837 to 1901. _____ (What?) were built during this time.
8 _____ (What?) was constructed to celebrate the end of the 20th century.

Unit 5 Lesson 1: Student A

3 Tell your partner your health problems, and give him / her advice about his / her problems.

1 Your dog has bitten my _____.
2 I've got an awful cold.
3 I fell off my bicycle and now my _____ is hurting badly.
4 I'm tired and stressed all the time.

A: *Your dog has bitten my* ___*finger*___ .
B: *Oh no! You should wash it straight away.*

Unit 5 Lesson 2: Student A

9 **Part 1**

1 You are a health club trainer. Ask your partner questions to complete this form.

ACTIVE FITNESS
Health Club

First name...........................
Surname..............................
Date of Birth......................
Occupation.........................
Diet......................................
Exercise..............................
Relaxation..........................

2 Give your partner two pieces of advice about how he / she can live more healthily.

Part 2

3 Read your role card. You want to join a health club. Answer Student B's questions.

You are Jo Lovejoy. You are 24 and you are a hairdresser. You eat a healthy diet, but you do very little exercise. You have a stressful life and only get about six hours' sleep a night.

4 Do you agree with the advice your partner gave you?

Unit 8 Lesson 1: Student A

2 Help your partner complete the article by explaining the words in green. Your partner will help you fill your spaces by giving you clues.

Breaking the Rules

Imagine a school where there are no (1) classrooms, no curriculum, no (2) _____ and no principal. There are no (3) _____ to send home to parents, no homework and no (4) tests to take at the end of term. At this school, students don't have to study unless they want to. Sounds impossible? Well, this is the reality for around 50 students who (5) _____ the Harrisburg Circle School in Pennsylvania, USA. Here, students are responsible for organising their own time and the teachers don't give (6) lessons unless students request them. So, if someone feels like learning French, (7) biology, or (8) _____, they can. If not, they can read a book, play a video game, cook, play the guitar or just hang out with friends. They can go outside whenever they want, although they can't leave the school grounds without (9) _____.

Students do have responsibilities, however. In the (10) morning every student has to sign up for a task, such as cleaning the floor, which they must do by the end of the day. Also, everyone has to attend the weekly school meetings, where all the (11) _____ about running the school are made.

There is a 'law book' which contains all the school rules about (12) behaviour, safety, and using school equipment. (13) Punishments for those who have (14) _____ the rules are decided in the weekly school meetings.

Some people question whether a school like this can provide a good (15) _____. But many of the school's students go on to get (16) degrees from colleges and universities all over the country, and abroad. Others go directly into the world of work. One ex-student who now runs a (17) successful T-shirt company said 'At this school I had to work things out for myself, and I could do it in my own time and in my own way. That (18) _____ me how to get what I want from life.' What more can you ask from a school?

Unit 12 Lesson 2: Student A

5 Read the advice and then prepare to report it to your partner using verbs like *said, warned, suggested, explained.*

Don't worry if you get held up and arrive a bit late, film sets are quite relaxed places. Don't speak to the stars unless they speak to you first, otherwise you could get fired. Take a book or a crossword because there will be a lot of waiting around and you will get bored. Make sure you fill in your form and hand it in before you leave, or you won't get paid.

Unit 3 Lesson 2: Student B

7 Ask your partner questions to complete the sentences.

1 _____ (Who?) built a city where London now stands. They called it Londinium.
   Who built a city where London now stands?
2 The Tower of London was built in the 11th century by _____ (Who?).
3 _____ (When?), houses in London were made of wood.
4 _____ (When?), ships were sent from London to explore the world.
5 A theatre called _____ (What?) was built in London during this time. Plays by Shakespeare were performed here.
6 In 1666, a fire started in a bread shop. _____ (How much?) of the city of London was destroyed.
7 Queen Victoria ruled from _____ to _____ (When?). The Houses of Parliament and Big Ben were built during this time.
8 The London Eye was constructed to celebrate _____ (Why?).

Unit 5 Lesson 1: Student B

3 Tell your partner your health problems, and give him / her advice about his / her problems.

1 Your dog has bitten my _____ .
2 I'm having a nose-bleed.
3 I can't sleep at night.
4 A horse has kicked my _____ .

A: *Your dog has bitten my* __**finger**__ .
B: *Oh no! You should wash it straight away.*

Unit 5 Lesson 2: Student B

9 **Part 1**

1 Read your role card. You want to join a health club. Answer Student A's questions.

You are Alex Fanshawe. You are 32 and you are a firefighter. You love sport and do a lot of exercise. You have a very busy social life and do not enjoy cooking. You often eat fast food.

2 Do you agree with the advice your partner gave you?

Part 2

3 You are a health club trainer. Ask your partner questions to complete this form.

ACTIVE FITNESS
Health Club

First name.............................
Surname...............................
Date of Birth.........................
Occupation...........................
Diet.......................................
Exercise................................
Relaxation.............................

4 Give your partner two pieces of advice about how he / she can live more healthily.

Unit 8 Lesson 1: Student B

2 Help your partner complete this text by explaining the words in green. Your partner will help you fill your spaces by giving you clues.

Breaking the Rules

Imagine a school where there are no (1) _____, no curriculum, no (2) timetables and no principal. There are no (3) reports to send home to parents, no homework and no (4) _____ to take at the end of term. At this school, students don't have to study unless they want to. Sounds impossible? Well, this is the reality for around 50 students who (5) attend the Harrisburg Circle School in Pennsylvania, USA. Here, students are responsible for organising their own time and the teachers don't give (6) _____ unless students request them. So, if someone feels like learning French, (7) _____, or (8) mathematics, they can. If not, they can read a book, play a video game, cook, play the guitar or just hang out with friends. They can go outside whenever they want, although they can't leave the school grounds without (9) permission.

Students do have responsibilities, however. In the (10) _____ every student has to sign up for a task, such as cleaning the floor, which they must do by the end of the day. Also, everyone has to attend the weekly school meetings, where all the (11) decisions about running the school are made.

There is a 'law book', which contains all the school rules about (12) _____, safety, and using school equipment. (13) _____ for those who have (14) broken the rules are decided in the weekly school meetings.

Some people question whether a school like this can provide a good (15) education. But many of the school's students go on to get (16) _____ from colleges and universities all over the country, and abroad. Others go directly into the world of work. One ex-student who now runs a (17) _____ T-shirt company said 'At this school I had to work things out for myself, and I could do it in my own time and in my own way. That (18) taught me how to get what I want from life.' What more can you ask from a school?

Unit 12 Lesson 2: Student B

5 Read the advice and then prepare to report it to your partner using verbs like *said*, *warned*, *suggested*, *explained*.

Bring your friend or your pet with you. They may be needed in the scene and if not they can keep you company while you are waiting to be called onto the set. Before you go, find out what kind of clothes you should wear. Bring a camera – you might get some good pictures of the stars.

Exam Guide

General Tips

When you do PET, you will get a question paper and an answer sheet.

This is a question paper: This is an answer sheet:

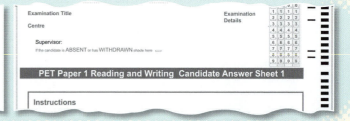

PRELIMINARY ENGLISH TEST

PAPER 1 Reading and Writing

TIME   1 hour 30 minutes

You can make notes on the question paper. For example, you can make notes while you listen, or you can underline parts of the reading texts.

You must write your answers in pencil on the answer sheet, so make sure you leave enough time to do this. At the end of the Listening paper you will have six minutes to transfer your answers to the answer sheets, but there is no extra time for the Reading and Writing paper.

For some questions, you need to put a mark below a letter, like this:

• Fill in your answers carefully and rub out any mistakes.
• Only choose one answer.

For some questions, you need to write a word, like this:

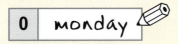

• Write your answers clearly, so the examiner can easily read them.
• There may be some words that you are not expected to know in the reading or listening texts. However, you will not be tested on these words.
• Check your spelling.

Reading • Part 1

What do I have to do?

• You have to read five very short texts and choose the correct answer, A, B or C, for each one.
• The texts may be signs, labels, notices, messages, notes, postcards, emails, or text messages.
• The texts are all separate and each one is on a different topic.

How do I do it?

• First read the instructions and look at the example.
• Read the first text and think about where you would see it. The appearance of the text may help with this. For example, it may be a sign on a shop window, a text message on a mobile phone, or a note on a kitchen table.
• Think about the meaning of the text and try to work out what the main message is.
• Read all three options carefully and decide which one matches the text best.
• When you have done this for all five texts, check your answers and then carefully transfer them to your answer sheet.

Over to you

Questions 1–5

Look at the text in each question.

What does it say?

Mark the correct letter **A**, **B**, or **C** on your answer sheet.

Example:

0
> Jo – your singing class
> is on Tuesday evening
> this week instead of
> Wednesday, starting an
> hour later than usual.

Jo's singing class

A will be a day earlier than normal.

B will not be in the evening this week.

C will no longer be on Wednesday.

Answer:

0	A	B	C
	■	☐	☐

1

Tennis lessons
In bad weather, table
tennis will take place in
the clubhouse instead.

A If it rains, a different activity will be available.

B The next tennis lesson has been cancelled due to bad weather.

C Tennis lessons may take place indoors or outdoors, depending on the weather.

2

> James – I loved that T-shirt
> you were wearing last
> night! Did you get it from
> a shop in town? I'd really
> like a similar one for
> myself. – Tamara

Tamara wants to know

A when James will wear his new T-shirt.

B which T-shirt James bought yesterday.

C where James bought his T-shirt.

3

From:	Simon
To:	Tim

I'm going camping with Eddie next
weekend. Do you want to join us?
If you do, we'll need to use your
big tent. Call me this evening.

Why did Simon write this email?

A to tell Tim about a change of plan

B to invite Tim on a camping trip

C to ask Tim to lend him a tent

4

ZIGGY'S
INTERNET CAFE

45 mins - $1.00
4 hours or more - $5.00

A There is a maximum charge of $5.00 to use the internet.

B You can use the internet for up to four hours at a time.

C If you wish to use the internet for more than 45 minutes speak to Ziggy.

5

Hi Kath,
I climbed this mountain yesterday.
It was hard work but the clouds
lifted when I got to the top so it
was worth it in the end!
Helen

A Helen regrets her decision to climb the mountain.

B Helen enjoyed climbing the mountain but couldn't see anything from the top.

C Although it was difficult, Helen was pleased she had climbed the mountain.

Reading • Part 2

What do I have to do?

- You have to read five short descriptions of people (6–10), and eight short texts (A–H).
- You have to match each person to the correct text. There will be three extra texts.
- The texts will be about things like books, courses, holidays, museums, websites.
- There may be some words that you are not expected to know in the texts. However, you will not be tested on these words.

How do I do it?

- Read the instructions to find the topic of the texts.
- Look at the descriptions of the people and underline the important information.
- Read the texts and find information that matches the descriptions of the people.
- The correct text will contain the same information as the description but in different words. It will meet all the requirements in the description, not just one or two of them.

Over to you

Questions 6–10

The people below all want to visit a museum.
On the opposite page there are descriptions of eight museums.
Decide which museum would be the most suitable for the following people.
For questions **6–10** , mark the correct letter **(A–H)** on your answer sheet.

6
John and Amanda are art lovers and want to spend the whole day at a museum. They'd like to have lunch there as well.

7
Sandra and Paulo want to take their two young children to a museum. The children are interested in nature and enjoy having things to do while they are in a museum.

8
Joachim is interested in learning how people used to live in the countryside. He doesn't want to pay too much to visit a museum and prefers places that aren't very crowded.

9
Gail wants to visit an old house that has exhibitions of furniture from the recent past. She would also like to spend some time outdoors and would enjoy seeing a concert or show.

10
Sebastian is an artist and would like the opportunity to improve his skills. He isn't keen on traditional museums but loves very old buildings and being outside.

Museums and Days Out

A   Bernley Museum

This museum shows how life was lived in Bernley when the village was one of the region's most important ports. There are lots of interesting objects and paintings, as well as art workshops and story-telling for children. It's best to go early as the museum is quite popular.

B   Granville Lodge

The Granville family lived here from 1635 until 1989, so this museum still feels like a family home. The living- and bedrooms are just as they were when the family moved out and the grounds are wonderful in spring and summer. Local music groups often play in the evenings.

C   Paul Roseby Museum

This museum houses the collection of Pierre Roseau, a 19th century traveller and scientist. It examines the way plants and animals have developed over the lifetime of the planet. There are workshops for younger visitors and experiments for them to try as they go around.

D   Flanton Castle

The grounds of this castle are free of charge but it's expensive to go inside. It's big enough to keep you busy all day, however, and there is a very nice restaurant. There are interesting exhibitions of clothes and furniture, but the quality of the artworks is a little disappointing.

E   Handier Abbey

The ruins of this ancient abbey are open every day and entrance is £5.00 per person. There are nature walks, literature talks and workshops on painting and drawing – but be warned that these are not suitable for beginners. The grounds are beautiful and the atmosphere is very peaceful.

F   City Museum

This museum is best known for its wonderful 17th and 18th century paintings and its sculptures. It will take you at least six hours to see everything so leave plenty of time. A new restaurant has just opened on the top floor, with great views of the city.

G   The Musical Farm

This is one of the most surprising and unusual museums in the region. Located in the heart of the countryside, it houses a collection of musical instruments. Children can try the drums and adults will enjoy watching the experts at work, making and repairing the instruments.

H   Careford Museum

This museum isn't well-known, so never gets terribly busy. Its 2,000 objects, including furniture, clothing and farm tools, create a picture of the traditional farming life of the region. There are regular performances of folk music. The entrance fee is reasonable and there's a restaurant serving delicious local food.

Reading • Part 3

What do I have to do?

- You have to read a longer, factual text and ten sentences (11–20).
- You have to decide if each sentence is correct (A) or incorrect (B).
- The sentences will come before the text and will be in the same order as the information in the text.

How do I do it?

- First read the instructions to find the topic of the text.
- Read the ten sentences so you know what information you have to look for.
- Read the text through quickly once.
- Look at the first sentence and underline the words in the text where you can find that information.
- Read that part of the text very carefully to decide if the sentence is correct or incorrect.
- The text and the sentence may contain the same information but in different words.

Over to you

Questions 11–20

Look at the sentences below about a garden gnome.
Read the text on the opposite page to decide if each sentence is correct or incorrect.
If it is correct, mark **A** on your answer sheet.
If it is not correct, mark **B** on your answer sheet.

---

11 Mrs Stuart-Kelso was upset about the theft of the gnome from her garden.

12 The contents of the parcel proved that the gnome had been to several continents.

13 In the letter, Murphy said that he came back because he was tired of travelling.

14 Mrs Stuart-Kelso asked a newspaper reporter to find out who had taken the gnome.

15 Simon's university friends had suggested taking the gnome.

16 There were a number of suitable gnomes for Simon to choose from.

17 Simon felt guilty about taking Mrs Stuart-Kelso's gnome.

18 Simon had problems at the borders of some countries he visited.

19 The Stuart-Kelsos considered reporting Simon to the police.

20 Simon has offered to repaint the gnome for Mrs Stuart-Kelso.

The Travelling Gnome

The story began when a garden gnome disappeared from the garden of Mrs Eve Stuart-Kelso. She noticed that it had gone and thought that someone had probably stolen it. Then she forgot all about it.

Seven months later however, she opened her front door and found the gnome, who she had named Murphy, on the doorstep. Beside him was a tightly wrapped parcel. Inside, Mrs Stuart-Kelso found a beautiful photo album showing Murphy doing various exciting activities at locations all over the world. There were pictures of the gnome mountain-climbing, standing in the mouth of a shark, swimming, and riding a motorbike. There was also a piece of paper with immigration stamps from the twelve countries the gnome had visited, which included Australia, South Africa, Thailand and Vietnam.

The parcel also contained a letter from the gnome. It said he had got bored sitting in Mrs Stuart-Kelso's garden all day long and had gone in search of adventure.

A journalist from a national newspaper heard about the story and set out to discover the identity of the person who had organised Murphy's travels. It was a law student called Simon Randles, who said he got the idea of travelling with the gnome when he was having a discussion with university friends about a French film they had seen. 'It was incredibly hard to find a gnome,' he said, 'but I was on a bus and saw this gnome in the garden'. He came back later that evening and "borrowed" him. He did feel a bit bad about it, he said, which is why he produced the album. He wanted the gnome's owners to have some great photos. He said the gnome was very useful on the trip and helped him to make friends with a lot of people. But it was difficult getting it through customs as the officials kept demanding to examine it!

Simon went to see Mr and Mrs Stuart-Kelso and told them all about his adventures with Murphy. They were fascinated by his story. 'It was the strangest gift I ever received,' said Mrs Stuart-Kelso. 'It makes me smile to see all the people he met on his travels. And it's so nice to get some good news.'

Mrs Stuart-Kelso said she did not want the police involved but warned Simon not to do it again. The gnome is now back in her garden. Its feet were slightly damaged during some of its adventures, which Simon apologised for, but her grandchildren are looking forward to giving it a coat of paint.

Reading • Part 4

What do I have to do?

- You have to read a text and understand both facts and people's attitudes and opinions.
- There are five multiple-choice questions (21–25), each with four options.
- Question 21 usually tests the writer's purpose, and question 25 asks about the writer's opinion. Both of these will test your understanding of the whole text.
- In questions 22–24, two questions test detailed meaning and one tests opinion or attitude. They will be in the same order as the information in the text.

How do I do it?

- Read the text once quickly to get an idea of the topic, then again for more detail.
- In questions 21 and 25, ask yourself the question, then look at the options to see which one matches your answer. Check the text again to make sure it is correct.
- Do questions 22, 23 and 24 one at a time, checking your answers against the text. Don't just match words in the text with the options. Think carefully about the meaning.

Over to you

Questions 21–25

Read the text and questions below.
For each question, mark the correct letter **A, B, C** or **D** on your answer sheet.

School of Rock

When Francis Seriau started giving drum lessons in his living room in 1983, people laughed at the idea of qualifications in pop music. But now he is head of a music school that has become a respected part of the British musical scene.

Seriau's Tech Music Schools in west London run a range of degree and diploma courses, including drums, guitar, keyboard and voice. More than 800 students are enrolled, some of them from as far away as Japan, Australia and Latin America. The classrooms are in a collection of old buildings and have the atmosphere of a university. Every available room is in use, with classes ranging from guitar technique through rock studies to business skills.

Seriau says, 'We try to prepare musicians for the real world by teaching practical things.' Students learn how to read music and how to manage their finances. Seriau explains that skilled musicians can earn far more than many people in supposedly 'safer' professions. The music world is changing all the time, however, and to make a career in it, students have to be ready to change too. Seriau aims to turn out musicians with the skills to succeed in this fast-moving industry.

Tech Music has not yet produced a major solo star, but a number of former pupils are members of top-level bands, for example Radiohead, Basement Jaxx and Massive Attack. Although not all students will become rich and famous, they graduate with a good musical training and realistic plans for the future. 'I had to sell my house to pay for the course,' says one student, who has just completed a one-year drum diploma, 'but it's been worth it. I've learned proper professional music skills and have just got my dream job, playing in a London musical.'

21 What is the writer trying to do in this text?

    A persuade people to take up jobs in music

    B explain how attitudes to pop music have changed

    C describe the career of a rock musician

    D explain the advantages of a good musical education

22 What do we learn about Tech Music Schools?

    A The teaching rooms are very modern.

    B They offer places to students from abroad.

    C The courses are limited to playing instruments.

    D There are plenty of practice rooms available.

23 Francis Seriau believes his students should

    A have an understanding of financial matters.

    B want to earn large amounts of money.

    C concentrate on their playing technique.

    D learn to play several different instruments.

24 What does the former drum student say?

    A He regrets having sold his house.

    B He is looking forward to his new employment.

    C He studied for several years at Tech Music.

    D He has enrolled for another course.

25 What would an advertisement for Tech Music Schools include?

    A *We teach a range of music and business courses and have schools on five continents.*

    B Enjoy learning, using the latest facilities in this newly-built music school.

    C **We'll teach you all you need to know to get a good job in the music industry.**

    D **Many of our former students are now major international stars. Study at *Tech Music Schools* and you can be one too!**

Reading • Part 5

What do I have to do?

- You have a short text with ten spaces (26–35) and an example (0).
- There are four multiple-choice word options for each space. You have to choose the correct option for each space.
- This part tests vocabulary, and some grammar.

How do I do it?

- Read the title and the text to get an idea of the topic.
- Go back to the beginning and think about the example.
- Work through the questions, looking at the words before and after each space.
- Try to think of a possible word for the space before you read the four options.
- Try all the options in the space to see if they are possible.
- Read the whole sentence to check that the word you have chosen makes sense.
- When you have completed the task read the whole text with your answers again.

Exam Extra!

Word sets

The words tested in each question will have similar meanings and be the same part of speech. Most of the words test your knowledge of vocabulary.

1 Read the sentences and try to think of a word to fill each space.

  1 This area of the coast is _____ as Shipwreck point.

  2 The necklace was of great _____ to my mother.

  3 Ice cream _____ of milk, sugar, eggs and cream.

  4 You will often see large groups of birds flying together during cold _____.

  5 Interestingly, _____ the houses look very different from the outside, they are very similar inside.

  6 Climate change will affect people in _____ part of the world.

2 Now look at the four options and the clue for each space, and choose your answer. Is it the word you first thought of?

  1 A told   B known   C called   D named
    (Clue: Which can be used with *as*?)

  2 A fee   B cost   C value   D charge
    (Clue: Which can mean *importance*?)

  3 A contains B consists C includes D involves
    (Clue: Which is always used with *of*?)

  4 A season   B climate   C weather   D temperature
    (Clue: Which is an uncountable noun?)

  5 A if   B since   C unless   D although
    (Clue: Which is used to link contrasting ideas?)

  6 A all   B any   C some   D every
    (Clue: Which can be used with a singular countable noun?)

Over to you

Questions 26–35

Read the text below and choose the correct word for each space.
For each question, mark the correct letter **A, B, C** or **D** on your answer sheet.

Example:

0   **A**   would   **B**   do   **C**   are   **D**   will

Answer:
0	A	B	C	D
	■	☐	☐	☐

Sugar gliders

How **(0)** _____ you like a sugar glider as a pet? As **(26)** _____ as their cute brown eyes and **(27)** _____ grey fur, these 20-centimetre-long animals from Australia have an unusual skill – they can fly. Sugar gliders have a **(28)** _____ of skin on their backs, which unfolds into a square **(29)** _____ a kite or a handkerchief. This **(30)** _____ them to 'fly' between branches as they search for food.

But **(31)** _____ a sugar glider might seem like a great pet, they need a lot of care and attention. To **(32)** _____ one at home you'll have to provide a diet of fruit, vegetables and baby cereal mixed **(33)** _____ warm water, honey and boiled eggs.

You'll **(34)** _____ have to stay up at night so your pet can fly around and you are **(35)** _____ to carry your sugar glider in a little bag around your neck so that it can get to know you.

26	**A** much	**B** well	**C** long	**D** often
27	**A** soft	**B** weak	**C** gentle	**D** calm
28	**A** part	**B** slice	**C** piece	**D** side
29	**A** as	**B** like	**C** for	**D** with
30	**A** lets	**B** makes	**C** allows	**D** creates
31	**A** whether	**B** unless	**C** because	**D** although
32	**A** protect	**B** store	**C** keep	**D** guard
33	**A** with	**B** by	**C** up	**D** round
34	**A** only	**B** too	**C** either	**D** also
35	**A** recommended	**B** suggested	**C** thought	**D** considered

Writing • Part 1

What do I have to do?

- There are five questions. The questions will all be on the same topic and may tell a story.
- For each question there will be two sentences. You must complete the second sentence so that it means exactly the same as the first.
- You may use no more than three words to complete the sentence.
- Your spelling must be correct in this part.

How do I do it?

- Read the instructions and the example. They will tell you the topic of the task.
- For each question, read the first sentence very carefully.
- Look at the second sentence and think how you can complete it so that it means exactly the same as the first sentence.
- When you have written all your answers, go back and check that you have not made any mistakes with grammar or spelling.

Over to you

Questions 1–5

Here are some sentences about a young tennis player.
For each question, complete the second sentence so that it means the same as the first.
Use no more than three words.
Write only the missing words on your answer sheet.
You may use this page for any rough work.

Example:

0 My 15-year-old brother plays tennis very well.

My 15-year-old brother .... **at playing tennis.**

Answer: | **0** | is very good |

---

1 He started having tennis lessons at the age of three.

He started having tennis lessons .... **was three.**

2 His teacher said he would be a champion one day.

His teacher said, '... **be a champion one day.'**

3 My brother wants to be successful, so he trains hard.

My brother trains hard .... **he wants to be successful.**

4 He can't go out with his friends as often as he'd like.

He'd like to go out with his friends .... **often.**

5 The last match he lost was six months ago.

He .... **a match for six months.**

Exam Extra!

Language often tested in Writing Part 1

Many different structures can be tested in Writing Part 1. Here are some examples.
Complete the second sentence so that it means the same as the first. Use no more
than three words.

Present perfect and past simple

1 I started supporting this football team six years ago.

   I _____ this team for six years.

Modal verbs

2 You are advised to take regular breaks when playing computer games.

   You _____ take regular breaks when playing computer games.

Active and passive

3 Three students were chosen by the coach to play in the match.

   The coach _____ three students to play in the match.

First conditional

4 If the bus isn't late, I'll be home at six.

   I'll be home at six unless the bus _____ late.

Reported speech

5 The teacher asked us if we wanted to have a class party.

   The teacher said, '_____ to have a class party?'

Possessives

6 I met one of my friends in the park yesterday.

   I met a friend of _____ in the park yesterday.

Comparisons and superlatives

7 My new scooter is much faster than my old one.

   My old scooter isn't _____ my new one.

Conjunctions

8 I left the house late but I still arrived at the party on time.

   I arrived at the party on time _____ I left the house late.

too / enough

9 It's too cold to play tennis outside today.

   It's not _____ to play tennis outside today.

so / such

10 It was such a beautiful day we decided to go out for a picnic.

   The weather was _____ beautiful that we decided to go out for
   a picnic.

Writing • Part 2

What do I have to do?

- You have to write a short message of between 35 and 45 words.
- The instructions will tell you who you are writing to and why.
- There will be three points which you must include in your message.
- You mustn't include any unnecessary information.

How do I do it?

- Read the question carefully so that you know what the situation is and why you are writing the message. Decide whether you need to write about the past, present or future.
- Plan your message. Remember, it must include the three content points asked for in the question.
- Keep your answer within the word limit. If you write too much you may include unnecessary information. If you write too little, you may miss one of the content points.
- When you have finished, check your answer carefully for mistakes with spelling and grammar.

Over to you

Question 6

There is a concert in the park near where you live, and you are going there on Sunday.

Write an email to your friend Jerome. In your email, you should

- invite Jerome to go to the concert with you

- explain what kind of concert it is

- say why you want to go there.

Write **35 to 45 words** on your answer sheet.

How does it work?

1 **Read these example answers to Part 2 and answer the questions below.**

    1 Which answer is too short?
    2 Which answer contains all three content points?
    3 Which answer talks about the past instead of the future?
    4 Which answer is missing one content point?
    5 Which answer has no punctuation?

1

> Dear Jerome,
>
> Would you like to go for a concert with me on Saturday? It's pop music
> concert and there will be lot of great bands there. I really want to go
> because of my favourite singer is performing there.
> Your friend
> Helena

2

> Hi Jerome
> There's a rock concert next weekend it looks really interesting because some
> famous musician will play. That's why I want to go. I hope you are well, see you
> at school tomorrow.
> Bye
> Maria

3

> Hello Jerome
> I went really good concert at weekend was classic music I like very much
> what your favourite concert

2 **Correct the mistakes in the exam answers.**

Writing • Part 3

What do I have to do?

- In Part 3 you choose whether to write a letter (question 7) or a story (question 8).
- You have to write about 100 words.
- For the story question, you may be given a title, or the opening words of the story.
- For the letter, you will have part of a friend's letter to reply to. This will give you the topic and one or two questions to answer.

How do I do it?

- Read question 7 and question 8 and decide which one interests you most.
- Remember, you only have to answer ONE of these questions.
- If you choose the letter, answer all the questions in the letter. Begin with *Dear* or *Hi* and end with an expression such as *best wishes*, *see you soon*, or *lots of love*.
- If you choose the story, make sure yours is clearly linked to the title or sentence. You will lose marks if the examiner cannot see how your story follows from the opening sentence, or if it is on a different subject from the title you were given.
- Do not write too few or too many words. If you write too few you will lose marks and if you write too many you have more chance of including unnecessary information and making mistakes.

How does it work?

1 Read the answers to questions 7 and 8 on page 84. Use the checklist below to say what is good and bad about the answers.

2 Correct the mistakes in the answers.

Checklist for Writing Part 3

☐ Does the answer have the correct number of words?

☐ Are verb tenses used correctly?

☐ Do the sentences start with a variety of different words?

☐ Are punctuation and capital letters used correctly?

☐ Are there any spelling mistakes?

☐ Are the sentences linked together?

☐ Does the answer show a range of structures and vocabulary?

☐ Does the answer stay on the topic of the question?

☐ If the answer is a story, does it have a beginning, middle and end?

☐ If the answer is a letter, does it open and close with a suitable expression?

Over to you

Write an answer to **one** of the questions (**7** or **8**) in this part.
Write your answer in about **100 words** on your answer sheet.
Put the question number in the box at the top of your answer sheet.

_____

Question 7

- This is part of a letter you receive from an English penfriend.

> I'm not sure what to do in the school holidays. My uncle has offered me a job in his bookshop, but I don't know if I want to work all summer! I know you worked in a shop last summer. What was it like? What do you think I should do?

- Now write a letter, answering your penfriend's questions.

- Write your **letter** on your answer sheet.

Question 8

- Your English teacher has asked you to write a story.

- This is the title for your story:

  ### The unopened box

- Write your **story** on your answer sheet.

Question 7

1   Dear Mark,

Yes, I had job in shop last sumer and I love it. It was sheo shop in town centre. I must
work long hours but I know some really nice people and I make lot of money. I will use
to buy car when I go to colege next year. You have lucky that your uncle has a shop. I
think you should working with your uncle. If you do you will saving money too. If you not
work you get bored because the sumer hollidays is quite long.

Let me know your desision, best wishes

Jack

2   Dear Hayley,

I don't know what to do in my school holidays. I might go and stay with my cousin in
the mountains he had a really nice house there. Or maybe I stay here and try find a
job. I don't know about working in a book shop I didn't ever worked in a book shop. If you
work you get tired and maybe have not time for fun on the beach.

Question 8

1   It was my birthday last week. I had a party and I got a lots of presents. I put all the
presents in my bedroom. I opened the presents after my party. I got nice presents.
I liked the presents. I said thank you to everyone. In two weeks later the phone
rang. It was my grandmother. She said me, 'Did you like your present?' I was very
embarrassing. I didn't know about a present from my grandmother. I went upstairs
and looked in my bedroom. Under the bed it was a little box. I pulled it and opened it. It
was a beautiful necklace from my grandmother. I loved it.

2   When I was a child I was very interested in a small, gold box that sat in our living room.
I asked my parents about it and they told me that my father had found it when he
was digging in the garden. No one could open it because it was locked and we didn't
have the key. For a few years I forgot all about it. Then one day I was helping my father
do some gardening. Suddenly I saw something shining. It was a tiny key. My father
and I looked at each other. Amazingly, we had found the key to the little box in the
living room!

Listening Paper • General Tips

- Don't worry if you don't get the answer at first. You will hear the recording twice, so you can try again the second time.
- Check your answers during the second playing. If you are still not sure about an answer, make a guess. Never leave a blank.
- As you listen, make notes on the question paper. There will be some time at the end of the listening test for you to transfer your answers to the answer sheet.

Listening • Part 1

What do I have to do?

- You will hear seven short conversations or monologues.
- These may be conversations between friends or family, or between customers and shop assistants. They may be extracts from radio or TV, recorded messages or talks.
- The texts are all separate and each one is on a different topic.
- There will be a question for each text (1-7) and three pictures, A, B and C.
- You have to listen and choose the picture which gives the best answer to the question.

How do I do it?

- There will be a short pause before each question, so read the question to find out what information you are listening for. You will also hear the question.
- Look at the pictures and think about the words you might hear.
- Think about the meaning of the text and try to work out the main message.
- Don't choose an answer just because you hear a word which appears in one of the pictures. All three pictures will be mentioned but only one will answer the question correctly.

What do I hear?

Here is the transcript for the example:

WOMAN:	Oh no! I haven't got my mobile!
MAN:	But you used it just now to book a table at the restaurant.
WOMAN:	Oh, I remember. I put it down on the steps while I put my coat on.
MAN:	Well, let's walk back quickly – it might still be there.

Questions 1–7

There are seven questions in this part.
For each question there are three pictures and a short recording.
Choose the correct picture and put a tick (✓) in the box below it.

Example: Where did the woman leave her mobile?

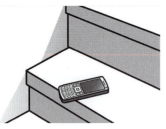

A ✓   B ☐   C ☐

---

1 What time will they meet tomorrow?

A ☐   B ☐   C ☐

2 What has William Long done most recently?

A ☐   B ☐   C ☐

3 What sport did Steve do on holiday?

A ☐   B ☐   C ☐

4 How will the boy get to the cinema?

A ☐

B ☐

C ☐

5 What's the earliest appointment the woman can offer Fiona Green?

A ☐

B ☐

C ☐

6 What present does Luke decide to buy for Karen's birthday?

A ☐

B ☐

C ☐

7 What will the man buy?

A ☐

B ☐

C ☐

Listening • Part 2

What do I have to do?

- You will hear either one speaker giving information, or a radio interview.
- There will be six multiple-choice questions (8–13).
- These will be either a question and three possible answers, or the first part of a sentence with three possible endings.
- You have to listen and choose the correct answer (A, B or C) to each question.

How do I do it?

- Use the time before the recording starts to read the questions and underline the important words.
- You will hear the information you need in the same order as the questions.
- Don't choose an answer just because you hear the words in the recording. The answer to a question will have the same meaning as the recording but may use different words.

What do I hear?

Here is part of the transcript:

| INTERVIEWER: | Welcome, Joe Durrant. You made an amazing journey, travelling 3,000 kilometres across Europe on a skateboard. What made you decide to do it? |
| JOE: | Two years ago I was feeling bored with my job and was looking for a challenge. I heard about an organisation called Boardwalk that helps teenagers with difficulties. I'm good at skateboarding and I know Europe well, so I thought, why not raise money for Boardwalk by skateboarding through France to the Spanish capital Madrid – about 3,000 kilometres. |

Exam Extra!

Listening for words with similar meanings

The answer to a question may not have exactly the same words as the recording, but the meaning will be the same. For example, in Question 8 on page 89, option B says *young people*, but in the recording you hear *teenagers*.

Match the phrases from the questions with a phrase you might hear in the recording.

1	giving him equipment	A	*as a brake*
2	arranging the ferry crossing	B	*been busy writing a book*
3	transported his equipment	C	*carried the tents and luggage*
4	stayed behind him	D	*followed me*
5	to slow himself down	E	*going up the steep stony road*
6	climbing the mountain	F	*lost a wheel from my board*
7	damaged his skateboard	G	*provided a tent and sleeping bag*
8	took up a different challenge	H	*provided boat tickets*

 *Over to you*

Questions 8–13

You will hear a radio interview with a man called Joe Durrant, who is talking about a skateboard journey.

For each question, put a tick (✓) in the correct box.

8 What was the purpose of Joe's skateboard journey?

    A to improve his skateboarding skills ☐

    B to support an organization for young people ☐

    C to visit some new places in Europe ☐

9 How did one local business help Joe prepare for the trip?

    A by planning the route ☐

    B by giving him equipment ☐

    C by arranging the ferry crossing ☐

10 What did Joe's friends in the camper van do?

    A They transported his equipment. ☐

    B They helped him change his wheels. ☐

    C They stayed behind him all the way. ☐

11 Joe spoiled a pair of new trainers by

    A using them to slow himself down. ☐

    B wearing them in the snow. ☐

    C climbing the mountain in them. ☐

12 When Joe was in Barcelona, he

    A damaged his skateboard. ☐

    B injured his foot. ☐

    C lost his camera. ☐

13 After the trip ended, Joe

    A was offered a job by Boardwalk. ☐

    B felt rather disappointed. ☐

    C took up a different challenge. ☐

Listening • Part 3

What do I have to do?

- You will hear some information from one speaker about things like a course, a holiday, a journey or a visitor attraction.
- On the question paper you will have some notes on the talk, with six spaces (14-19).
- You have to listen and fill each space with a word or number from the listening.

How do I do it?

- Read the instructions and find out what the conversation will be about.
- Look at the form and think about the information you will be listening for. For example, you might need to listen for a day, a time, a price, a place or a telephone number.
- You might hear two possible answers (two times or two prices). Listen carefully to choose the right one.
- You should write the word exactly as you hear it. You will not be expected to change it in any way.
- You are expected to spell simple and very frequent words correctly. Write numbers as numbers (25) not words (twenty-five), so you don't make a mistake with the spelling.

What do I hear?

Here is part of the transcript:

> Superstars Drama School is offering two fantastic courses this summer. One is called Musical Theatre and the other is Comedy Acting – especially for those of you who are good at making people laugh. Our Screen Acting class, which is always popular, will return in the autumn.
>
> All of our teachers are professional actors who will give you individual attention and the best advice possible. Each course is 30 hours per week and runs for three weeks. If you book within the next two weeks you'll get a 10% discount.

 **23** *Over to you*

Questions 14-19

You will hear a man talking to a group of people about a drama school.

For each question, fill in the missing information in the numbered space.

Superstars Drama School

Summer courses: (14) _____ Acting

 Musical Theatre

Length of each course: (15) _____ weeks

Facilities: Video recording studio

 Beautiful garden

 Café serving drinks and (16) _____

Transport: bus numbers 62 or 381

 not advisable to come by (17) _____

Accommodation: Fifteen minutes walk from college

 Close to several (18) _____

 Students must provide (19) _____ for the beds

 Housekeeper's name is Mrs Russell

Website address: www.superstars.co.uk

Listening • Part 4

What do I have to do?

- You will hear a conversation between two people, usually a male and a female.
- They will talk about and give their opinions on a subject. They may agree and disagree with each other, and they will reach a conclusion at the end.
- The six questions (20-25) are sentences about the attitudes and opinions of the speakers.
- You have to listen and decide if the sentences are correct (A) or incorrect (B).

How do I do it?

- Before the recording starts, read the instructions to find out who the speakers are and what they will talk about.
- Read the six sentences and underline the words that show attitude and opinion, for example *think*, *agree*, *suggest*, *believe*.
- Underline the topic of each sentence. The words you hear in the recording will not be exactly the same as the words in the sentences.
- You will hear the information you need in the same order as the questions.
- As you listen to the recording, decide if the sentences are correct (A) or incorrect (B).

Exam Extra!

Reporting verbs

The sentences often include a reporting verb that sums up what one of the speakers says. Match the statements to the reporting verbs.

admire admit doubt regret suggest warn

1 I know the film got terrible reviews and it was quite silly, but actually I really enjoyed it! _____

2 What about entering your pictures in a photography competition? _____

3 I think it's very unlikely that I'd win a prize. _____

4 That's a really cool T-shirt – where did you get it? _____

5 I spent all weekend writing that essay and I still only got a *C* for it. What a waste of time! _____

6 If you carry your wallet in your back pocket like that it might get stolen! _____

What do I hear?

Here is part of the transcript:

STEVE:	Hi Claire. You look a bit depressed. What's the matter?
CLAIRE:	Hi Steve. Well, it's my dad. I'm really annoyed with him. I hate it when we get cross with each other but you'll never believe what he's done.
STEVE:	Well go on, tell me. What has he done?
CLAIRE:	Well you know my mum is always telling me to tidy my bedroom? Dad's only gone and posted a picture of my untidy room on his website. I'm so embarrassed. I'm 20 and I've got a job and he's acting as if I'm still a little kid.

 **24** *Over to you*

Questions 20–25

Look at the six sentences for this part.

You will hear a conversation between a boy, Steve, and a girl, Claire, about Claire's room.

Decide if each sentence is correct or incorrect.

If it is correct put a tick (✓) in the box under **A** for **YES**. If it is not correct put a tick (✓) in the box under **B** for **NO**.

		A YES	B NO
20	Claire dislikes having arguments with her father.	☐	☐
21	Claire feels that her father has acted reasonably.	☐	☐
22	Claire has refused to do what her father wants.	☐	☐
23	Steve thinks that lots of people will see Claire's room online.	☐	☐
24	Steve suggests Claire should stop living at home.	☐	☐
25	Steve warns Claire that she might not like his sister.	☐	☐

The Speaking Test

About the Speaking Test

- The Speaking Test takes between ten and twelve minutes.
- You do the test with a partner, or occasionally in a group of three.
- There are two examiners. One will ask questions, the other will just listen.

Exam Extra!

What do I do if I don't understand?

If you don't understand a question, you can ask for help. Look at these phrases.

1 Can you say that again, please?

2 What does (that word) mean?

3 Could you repeat that please?

4 Can you speak louder please?

5 Could you say that more slowly?

Which questions should you ask if:

A you can't hear what someone said?

B you do not understand a word?

C someone is speaking too quickly?

Speaking • Part 1

What do I have to do?

- You have to answer the examiner's questions.
- The questions are about your life – your daily life, your family, hobbies, likes and dislikes.
- You will have to spell your name or a word from your address for one of the questions.
- In this part you talk to the examiner, not your partner.
- The examiner also asks your partner some questions.
- This part of the test takes 2–3 minutes.

How do I do it?

- Listen carefully, because the examiner will not ask you the same questions as your partner.
- Speak clearly so the examiners and your partner can hear you.
- If you don't understand a question, ask the examiner to repeat it.
- Try to give full answers and add some extra information to make your answers interesting.

What do you enjoy doing in your free time?

I like playing sports.

I like doing sports. I play basketball once a week, and tennis twice a week.

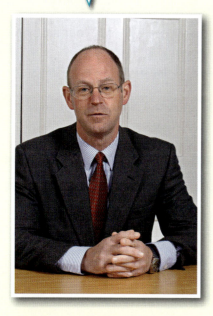

Speaking • Part 2

What do I have to do?

- In this part you talk to your partner, not the examiner.
- The examiner will describe a situation to you. You have to discuss the possibilities and reach a decision. You should be able to make suggestions, agree and disagree.
- The examiner will give you a sheet of paper with some pictures to help you.
- You will hear the instructions twice.
- This part will take about 2-3 minutes.

How do I do it?

- Make sure you understand what you have to do. Check with the examiner if you are not sure.
- Take turns to talk about each picture with your partner. Listen to what your partner says and agree or disagree with it.
- Make sure you talk about all of the pictures, and don't forget to ask your partner questions.
- Try not to reach a decision too quickly – you need to show the examiner that you can make suggestions, agree and disagree.

Exam Extra!

Discussing options

1 *What about … ?*

2 *I think this would be good because … .*

3 *I'm not sure about … .*

4 *That's a good idea but … .*

5 *What do you think about … ?*

Which of these phrases could you use to:

A make a suggestion?

B ask your partner's opinion?

C react to your partner's opinion?

How does it work?

I'm going to describe a situation to you. A classmate of yours has moved to another town and wants to make some new friends. Talk about the different things your friend could do to meet new friends, and decide which would be best.

Here is a picture with some ideas to help you.

I'll say that again. A classmate of yours …

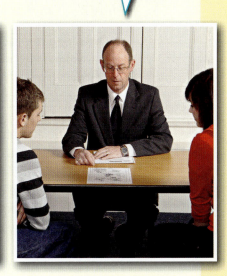

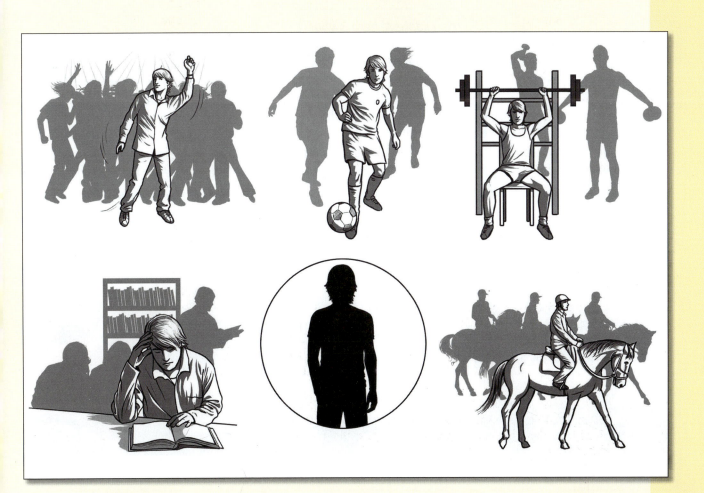

Speaking • Part 3

What do I have to do?

- In this part you talk to the examiner, not your partner.
- The examiner will give you a photograph of an everyday situation and ask you to talk about it.
- After about one minute, the examiner will take your photograph back and ask your partner to describe a different picture, on the same topic.
- This part will take about three minutes.

How do I do it?

- Think for a few seconds before you start to talk about the picture.
- The examiner wants to see how much vocabulary you know and how well you can express yourself, so describe the picture as fully as you can.
- Imagine you're describing the photograph to someone who can't see it. Talk about all of the people and activities you see. Add details about clothes, the weather, colours, objects etc.
- Don't worry if you don't know the word for something in the picture – try to explain it using phrases like *You use it to* (+ infinitive), *It's used for* (+ -ing), *It looks as if ...* , *The thing you use when ...*
- Try to keep talking until the examiner stops you.
- Listen when it is your partner's turn to talk.

How does it work?

Now, I'd like each of you to talk on your own about something. I'm going to give each of you a photograph of people packing.

Candidate A, here is your photograph. Please show it to Candidate B, but I'd like you to talk about it.
Candidate B, you just listen. I'll give you your photograph in a moment.
Candidate A, please tell us what you can see in your photograph.

Now, Candidate B, here is your photograph. It also shows people packing. Please show it to Candidate A and tell us what you can see in the photograph.

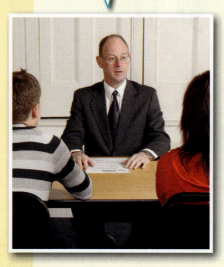
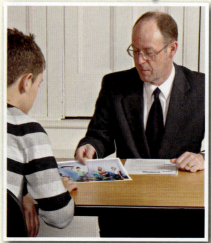
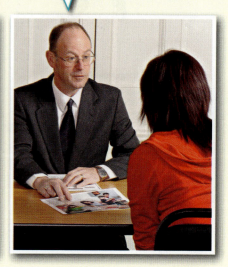

Candidate A

Candidate B

Speaking • Part 4

What do I have to do?

- In this part, you have a conversation with your partner.
- The examiner will tell you what to talk about but will not take part in the conversation.
- The topic will be the same as the theme of the photographs in Part 3.
- You should talk together until the examiner stops you.
- This part will take about three minutes.

How do I do it?

- Make sure that you both take an equal part in the conversation.
- Talk about your interests and opinions, and give reasons for them.
- Don't talk for too long and ask questions to give your partner a chance to speak.
- Listen to what your partner says and show that you are interested.

How does it work?

Your pictures showed people packing. Now, I'd like you to talk together about the different times when you have had to do packing, and the different kinds of things you packed.

Thank you. That's the end of the test.

PET Language summary

Unit 1

Verbs of like and dislike

We use these verbs to talk about things we like and don't like.

100%   0%

love enjoy quite like don't mind hate /can't stand

- *I love animals!*
- *I can't stand that man!*

We can use a noun or *–ing* form of a verb after these verbs.

- *I enjoy tennis.*
- *I quite like playing basketball.*
- *I hate shopping!*

Present simple

+		I / You / We / They	work.
		He / She / It	works.
-		I / You / We / They	don't work.
		He / She / It	doesn't work.
?	Do	I / you / we / they	work?
	Does	he / she / it	work?

We use present simple …

- for things that happen regularly.
- *We often play tennis on Saturdays.*
- for long-term situations.
- *I live in Madrid.*
- with stative verbs (verbs that are not used in continuous tenses, e.g. *hate, have got, hear, know, like, remember, see, understand*).
- *I love dancing.*
- *I don't know him very well.*

Present continuous

+	I	am	working.
	He / She / It	is	working.
	You / We / They	are	working.
-	I	'm not	working.
	He / She / It	isn't	working.
	You / We / They	aren't	working.
?	Am	I	working?
	Is	he / she / it	working?
	Are	you / we / they	working?

We use present continuous …

- for something we are doing now.
- *I'm watching TV at the moment.*
- for a short term situation.
- *He's staying with his aunt for a few weeks.*

be keen on, be good at and *be interested in*

We can also use some adjectives + prepositions to talk about things we like and don't like. They are followed by a noun or an *–ing* form of a verb.

- *I'm not keen on football.*
- *Are you interested in acting?*

We use *be good at* followed by a noun or an *–ing* form to talk about ability.

- *She's good at skiing.*

We can use adverbs to make these expressions stronger.

- *He's very good at tennis.*
- *I'm really keen on music.*

Unit 2

Comparative and superlative adjectives

Adjective	Comparative	Superlative
1 syllable:	+ -er	+ the -est
young	younger	the youngest
ending in -y:	y, + -ier	y, + the -iest
lazy	lazier	the laziest
2 syllables:	+ more / less	+ the most / least
handsome	more handsome	the most handsome
Irregular:		
good	better	the best
bad	worse	the worst

For long adjectives, we use *more* + *than* and *the most*. We can also use *less* + *than* and *the least*.

- *She's more confident than her sister.*
- *He is less good-looking than his brother* (= his brother is more good-looking).
- *She is the least hard-working in the family.*

We can also use *as ... as* to compare things.

- *He is as tall as his brother* (= they are the same height).
- *She's not as lazy as Matt* (= Matt is lazier than her).

so / such ... that

We use *so* and *such* for emphasis. We use *so* + adjective and *such (a)* + adjective + noun.

- *The room is so messy I can't find anything.*
- *I've never seen such a messy room.*

We use *so much / so many* to emphasize amount or number.

- *I've got so much work to do!*
- *There were so many people there!*

too / enough ... to

We can use *too* + adjective / adverb when there is more of something than we want.

- *The room is too small.*
- *He talks too quickly.*

We can use adjective / adverb + *enough* when there is as much as we need.

- *The music is loud enough* (= it's as loud as we need).
- *The room isn't big enough* (= it is too small).

We can also use *enough* + noun when an amount is satisfactory.

- *There is enough space for a desk.*

Extreme adjectives

Ordinary adjective	Extreme adjective
good	brilliant
bad	awful
surprising	amazing

Extreme adjectives have a stronger meaning than ordinary adjectives. We can't use *very* with extreme adjectives (they already mean *very* ...), but we can use *completely* or *absolutely*.

- *It was an absolutely amazing party!*
- *The DJ was completely awful!*

We can use *really* with both ordinary and extreme adjectives.

- *Janice's dancing was really good.*
- *The music was really brilliant!*

Describing people

We use *be* with adjectives

- *She is blonde / tall / cheerful.*

We use *have* or *have got* with nouns.

- *He's got brown hair / two brothers / a good sense of humour.*

Unit 3

Past simple

+	I did	my homework.
-	I didn't do	my homework.
?	Did you do	your homework?

We use past simple for actions or situations in the past. For regular verbs, we form past simple with *-ed*.

- *They cleaned the house yesterday.*

Some verbs are irregular:

- *do → did, find → found, get → got, have → had, be → was / were*

We use *did / didn't* + verb to form negatives and questions.

- *They didn't have electricity.*
- *Did they clean the house?*

used to

+	I		used to	work hard.
-	I		didn't use to	work hard.
?	Did	you	use to	work hard?

We use *used to* for situations or regular actions in the past.

- *They used to live in a big house.*
- *We used to get up early every day.*

In negatives and questions, we use *did(n't)* + *use to*.

- *I didn't use to like fish.*
- *Did you use to live in Madrid?*

We can't use *used to* for things that only happened once.

- *We played cards last night.*
- ~~*We used to play cards last night.*~~

Passive and active

Active	Passive
They make films in Hollywood.	Films are made in Hollywood.
They built the stadium in 2006.	The stadium was built in 2006.

For present simple passive, we use the present simple of *be* + past participle.

- *Coffee is grown in Brazil.*
- *Computers are used in schools.*

For the past simple passive, we use the past simple of *be* + past participle.

- *The cinema was destroyed by fire.*
- *These houses were built last year.*

We use the passive when the action of a sentence is more important than the subject.

- *Dickens wrote this book* (= active: the subject 'Dickens' is important).
- *This book was written in 1985* (= passive: the subject of the verb is not important).

owing to / due to

We use *owing to* and *due to* to give a reason.

- *The sports centre was never finished owing to a lack of money.*
- *We were late due to heavy traffic.*

Owing to and *due to* are followed by a noun; *because* is followed by a verb clause.

- *Our flight was cancelled due to bad weather.*
- *Our flight was cancelled because the weather was bad.*

Unit 4

Agreeing and disagreeing

We use these expressions to agree with someone.

- *Yes, you're right.*
- *That's a good / the best idea.*
- *What a good idea!*

We use these expressions to disagree politely.

- *Well, I'm not sure.*
- *I don't think that's a good idea.*

Suggesting

	Verb	
Let's	watch	a DVD.
How / What about	going	to the cinema?
Why don't we	go	to a restaurant?
I think we should	leave	now.

We use *Let's*, *How / What about*, *Why don't we* and *I think we should* to make suggestions.

Notice that after *How / What about* we use the *-ing* form of the verb.

- *How about going swimming?*

may / might / could

		Verb	
I	might	have	a party.
We	could	make	a cake.
They	may	help	us.

We use *may*, *might* and *could* to talk about things that will possibly happen.

- *It might rain tomorrow.*
- *We may be late.*

Quantifiers

Uncountable nouns	Countable nouns	Both
little	few	no
a little	a few	none of
much	a couple of	some
a great deal of	several	plenty of
	many	lots of
		most
		all of

We use quantifiers to talk about quantity.

We use *some* in affirmative sentences and offers, but we use *not any* in negative sentences.

- *He's got some CDs.*
- *Would you like some coffee?*
- *We haven't got any money.*

We use *much* and *many* in negative sentences and questions, but we use *a lot of* in affirmative sentences.

- *They haven't got much money.*
- *Has she got many friends?*
- *He's got a lot of CDs.*

Few and *little* refer to a very small quantity, but *a few* and *a little* refer to a slightly larger quantity.

- *He's got little money / few friends* (almost none).
- *He's got a little money / a few friends* (a small amount).

Unit 5

should / ought to

		Verb	
You	should	see	a doctor.
You	ought to	rest	for a few days.

We use *should* and *ought to* to give advice.

- *You should stay at home if you're ill.*
- *You ought to go to bed.*

The negative forms are *shouldn't* and *ought not to.*

- *You shouldn't go to school if you're ill.*
- *You ought not to go out in the cold.*

Adverbs and adverbial phrases

Adverbs are one word. Adverbial phrases usually have a preposition and a noun.

- *He smiled **happily**.*
- *He smiled **with delight**.*

Adverbs and adverbial phrases usually come after a verb.

Adverbs of manner tell us how something happens.

- *He walked **quickly**.*
- *She wrote **with a pencil**.*

Adverbs of manner can also come at the beginning of a sentence.

- ***Slowly**, she turned round.*

Adverbs of place tell us where something happens.

- *He ran **away**.*
- *She sat **by the door**.*

Adverbs of time tell us when something happens.

- *He phoned me **yesterday**.*
- *They arrived **in the morning**.*

When there is more than one adverb, the order is usually

manner – place – time

- *She walked slowly home later that evening.*

Forming adverbs

Adjective	Adverb
most adjectives	+ *ly*
normal	*normally*
adjectives ending in -*y*	~~y~~ + *ily*
easy	*easily*
adjectives ending in -*le*	~~e~~ + *y*
horrible	*horribly*

Some adjectives are irregular.

Adjective	Adverb
good	*well*
fast	*fast*
early	*early*

-ing and *-ed* adjectives

Adjectives ending in -*ing* tell us what something is like.

- *The film was boring.*
- *It was a very relaxing holiday.*

Adjectives ending in -*ed* describe how we feel.

- *I was bored all afternoon.*
- *I felt very relaxed on holiday.*

Unit 6

Past continuous and past simple

+	I / He / She / It	was	reading.
	You / We / They	were	reading.
-	I / He / She / It	wasn't	reading.
	You / We / They	weren't	reading.
?	Was	I / he / she / it	reading.
	Were	you / we / they	reading.

We use past continuous for an action in progress in the past.

* At nine o'clock yesterday I was watching TV.

We use past simple for a single event in the past.

* I went to the cinema last night.

We use past simple and past continuous together when a single event interrupts an action in progress.

* Sam was waiting for me when I got home.

We use *when* before past simple, and we use *while* before past continuous.

* She was driving home when the accident happened.
* The accident happened while she was driving home.

We use *when* + two verbs in past simple when one action happened after another. Compare:

* When we arrived, she cooked a meal (= we arrived, then she cooked a meal).
* When we arrived, she was cooking a meal (= she started cooking before we arrived).

Conjunctions

We use *as soon as*, *before*, *when*, *while* and *until* to link events and say when they happened.

* We went inside **as soon as** it started to rain (= it started to rain, then we went inside immediately).
* I put up the tent **while** he made a fire (= we did these things at the same time).
* We stayed there **until** it was dark (= it got dark, then we left).

We use *if* and *unless* to talk about things that might happen.

* The animals will die **unless** we help them (= if we don't help them).

We use *because*, *since* and *as* to give a reason.

* We didn't play tennis **because / as** it was raining.

We use *so that* to talk about purpose.

* I walked to work **so that** I could get some exercise.

We use *although*, *even though* and *but* to link contrasting ideas.

* They are poor, **but** they are happy.
* **Although** they are poor, they are happy.
* **Even though** they are poor, they are happy.

despite / in spite of

We use *despite* and *in spite of* to introduce a contrasting idea.

* We enjoyed our holiday **despite / in spite of** the bad weather.

Despite and *in spite of* are always followed by a noun.

* We swam in the sea **despite** the cold.
* NOT We swam in the sea **despite** it was cold.

Unit 7

Comparative and superlative adverbs

Adverb	Comparative	Superlative
Regular:	+ more ...	+ the most ...
quickly	more quickly	the most quickly
Irregular:		
well	better	the best
badly	worse	the worst
hard	harder	the hardest
far	further	the furthest
a lot	more	the most
not much	less	the least

We use comparative and superlative adverbs to compare the way people do things.

- *Sara works more quickly than I do.*
- *Who can swim the furthest?*

We use *than* after comparative adverbs.

- *He works harder than the others.*

We use *more, the most, less* and *the least to* compare how much someone does something.

- *I enjoy basketball more than football.*
- *I like swimming the least.*

We can use words like *much* and *a bit* to modify comparative adverbs.

- *Anna works much harder than I do.*
- *I can ski a bit better than I can snowboard.*

Present perfect and past simple

+	I / You / We / They	have	left.
	He / She / It	has	left.
-	I / You / We / They	haven't	left.
	He / She / It	hasn't	left.
?	Have	I / you / we / they	left?
	Has	he / she / it	left?

We form present perfect with *have* + past participle.

- *I have finished my homework.*
- *Tom has left.*

We use present perfect for something that happened at some time in the past.
We use past simple for something that happened at a definite time in the past.

- *I've met Rafael Nadal* (= at some time).
- *I met Rafael Nadal last year* (= at a definite time).

We use present perfect + *just* for something that happened in the recent past.

- *Sam's just left* (= a short time ago).

We use present perfect + *for / since* for something that started in the past and is still continuing.

- *I've lived here for five years* (= I still live here).

Present perfect with *for* and *since*

We use *for* and *since* with present perfect to say how long something has continued.

We use *for* + a period of time, and *since* + a specific time.

- *I have lived here for three years / two weeks / my whole life.*
- *I have lived here since 2004 / last week / I was seven.*

Unit 8

Obligation, prohibition and permission

	modal	verb	
You	have to	wear	a uniform.
You	must	arrive	on time.
You	mustn't	be	late.
You	can't	park	here.
You	don't have to	pay	for lessons.
You	needn't	study	music.
You	can	use	a calculator.

We use *have to* and *must* when something is necessary.

- *You must / have to wear a seat belt when you're driving.*

We use *mustn't* and *can't* when something is not allowed.

- *You mustn't / can't talk during the exam.*

We use *don't have to* and *needn't* when something is not necessary.

- *The concert is free – you needn't / don't have to pay.*

We use *can* when something is allowed.

- *You can learn to drive when you are 17.*

Compare *mustn't* and *don't have to*.

- *You mustn't bring food to school (= it's not allowed).*
- *You don't have to bring food to school (= it's not necessary).*

past obligation and permission

We use *had to* for obligation in the past, and *could* for permission in the past.

- *My dad had to wear a uniform at school.*
- *When I was at school, we could wear our own clothes.*

Relative pronouns

We use relative pronouns to join sentences together.

- *John is a boy. He lives near me.*
  → *John is a boy who lives near me.*

people:	who, that
things:	which, that
places:	where
time:	when
possession:	whose

We use *who* for people and *which* for things. We can use *that* for people or things.

- *She's the girl who / that Tom loves.*
- *That's the bike which / that I'd like to buy.*

We use *where* for places.

- *That's the house where Sara lives.*

We use *when* for times.

- *I remember the day when I started school.*

We use *whose* to talk about possession.

- *That's the boy whose mother is an actress (= his mother is an actress).*

Forming words for jobs

We often make words for jobs by adding suffixes to verbs or nouns.

We can add *-ist* to a noun.

art → artist
novel → novelist
guitar → guitarist
journal → journalist

We can add *-(e)r* or *-or* to a verb.

design → designer
farm → farmer
invent → inventor
direct → director

Unit 9

Predicting the future

	modal	verb	
Cars	will	use	less petrol.
Trains	could	be	cheaper.
We	may	have	more free time.
Robots	might	do	a lot of our work.

We use *will*, *could*, *may* and *might* to predict the future. *Will* is more certain than *could*, *may* and *might*.

- *There will be more pollution in the future* (= it's certain).
- *There might be space travel* (= it's possible).

The negative form of *will* is *won't*.

- *There won't be many fish in the sea in twenty years.*

We can modify *will* with adverbs like *probably* and *definitely*.

- *Cars will probably be cheaper.*
- *The earth will definitely be warmer.*

Adverbs come after *will* but before *won't*.

- *It will probably be quite cheap.*
- *It probably won't cost much.*

We can also use *be + likely / unlikely to* to make predictions.

- *Planes are likely to be faster* (= they will probably be faster).
- *Houses are unlikely to change much* (= they probably won't change).

First conditional and *unless*

If clause	main clause
If we play well,	we will win.
If we don't hurry up,	we will be late.

main clause	*if* clause
We will win	if we play well.
We will be late	if we don't hurry up.

We use first conditional to talk about things that are possible in the future. The verb in the *if* clause is in present tense.

- *If I see George, I'll tell him.*
- NOT *If I will see George, I'll tell him.*

We can also use *may*, *might*, *can* or *could* in the main clause.

- *If it's sunny, we might play tennis.*

We can use *unless* instead of *if* in conditional sentences. *Unless* means *if not*.

- *You won't pass the exam unless you study* (= you won't pass the exam if you don't study).

going to

We use *going to* for predicting the future when we can see evidence now of what is likely to happen.

- *The sky's very dark. I think it's going to rain* (= a prediction based on evidence now).
- *I think it will rain tomorrow* (= a general prediction).

We also use *going to* for plans and intentions.

- *I'm going to get a job in the summer holidays.*

Unit 10

Second conditional

if clause	main clause
If I won the lottery,	I would go travelling.
If you went to bed earlier,	you wouldn't be so tired.

main clause	if clause
I would go travelling	if I won the lottery.
You wouldn't be so tired	if you went to bed earlier.

We use second conditional to talk about imagined situations.

- *If I wasn't afraid of heights, I would visit the Empire State Building*
  (= I am afraid of heights so I won't).

We use past simple in the *if* clause, and we use *would / wouldn't* in the main clause.

- *If I had a lot of money, I wouldn't work.*

Would is often shortened to *'d'*.

- *If I had friends in America, I'd (= I would) go and visit them.*

We can put the *if* clause or the main clause first in the sentence. When the *if* clause comes first, we use a comma.

- *He'd get good marks if he worked harder.*
- *If he worked harder, he'd get good marks.*

We can also use *could* or *might* in the main clause instead of *would* if the result is not definite.

- *If you went on an adventure holiday, you might enjoy it.*

If I were you ...

We often use *were* instead of *was* in the *if* clause.

- *If I were rich, I'd buy a sports car.*

We can use *If I were you* to give advice.

- *If I were you, I'd take it back to the shop*
  (= you should take it back).

Second conditional questions

We can make *yes / no* questions in the second conditional by changing the order of the modal verb and the subject in the main clause.

- *If there was more time in the day, you would spend it sleeping.*
- *If there was more time in the day, would you spend it sleeping?*

We can make open questions in the second conditional by using a question word in the main clause. The modal verb comes before the subject.

- *If I came to your town, what could I see?*
- *If you had three wishes, how would you use them?*

We can put the if clause or the main clause first in the question. When the if clause comes first, we use a comma.

- *If you lost your passport on holiday, what would you do?*
- *What would you do if you lost your passport on holiday?*

Modal passives

	modal	be	past participle	
Tickets	can	be	bought	on the internet.
Cars	should	be	parked	in the car park.
Dogs	must	be	kept	on leads.

We form modal passives with a modal verb + *be* + past participle.

- *All tickets must be shown at the entrance gate.*

Modal passives are quite formal, and they are often used on signs and official notices.

- *Computers and mobile phones should be switched off during take-off and landing*
  (= on a plane).
- *Mobile phones must not be used in this part of the hospital* (= in a hospital).

Unit 11

Adjective order

opinion	lovely / wonderful / horrible
size	big / tiny / enormous
age	brand new / ancient / old
shape	round / square / triangular
colour	red / silver / greenish
pattern	stripy / spotted / flowery
material	woollen / silk / plastic

When there is more than one adjective before a noun, we use them in the order in the table above.

- *They've got a lovely old house.*
- *He was wearing a horrible brown jumper.*
- *She bought a beautiful black silk dress.*

When there are two colour adjectives before a noun, we use *and*.

- *He was wearing a blue and white shirt.*

When adjectives come after a noun, they can be in any order.

- *His clothes were old and dirty.*

Phrasal verbs to talk about clothes

With *try on*, *put on* and *take off*, we can put the object either before or after the preposition.

- *I **tried on** a lovely shirt, but it didn't fit.*
- ***Put** your coat **on** – it's really cold.*
- *If I **take off** my glasses, I can't see!*

With *wear out*, we can use an object pronoun before the preposition. We can also use the passive voice.

- *I **wore out** my trainers by running so much!*
- *I **wore** them **out** very quickly.*
- *These jeans are **worn out**. There are holes in the knees!*

With *go with*, the object must come after the preposition.

- *I bought a new scarf to **go with** my red boots.*

like and just like

Like means 'similar to'. We use *be* + *like* + noun.

- *Your shoes are like mine.*
- *This dress is like Maria's.*

Just like means 'exactly similar to'.

- *Your jacket is just like Sara's.*

We can also use *look* + *like* + noun.

- *Those boots look like my old ones.*

have / get something done

	have / get	noun	past participle	
She	has	her hair	cut	once a month.
I	get	my eyes	tested	every year.
We	had	the car	fixed	at the garage.

We use *have / get something done* when someone else does a job for us.

- *If you suffer from headaches, you should get your eyes tested (= ask someone to test them).*
- *We had the car fixed last week (= someone fixed it for us).*

Talking about money

We use *by* to talk about ways to pay a bill.

- *You can pay **by** cash or credit card, but not by cheque.*

We usually use *hire* for shorter periods and *rent* for longer periods or bigger items.

- *Have you bought your apartment or is it rented?*
- *Why don't we hire bikes for the afternoon?*

If you don't want something you have bought, you can *return* or *exchange* it.

- *My new laptop doesn't work so I'm going to return it and get my money back.*
- *This skirt I bought is the wrong size so I'd like to exchange it please.*

Unit 12

Past perfect

+	I / You / He / She / It / We / They	had	worked.
-	I / You / He / She / It / We / They	hadn't	worked.
?	Had	I / you / he / she / it / we / they	worked?

We form past perfect with *had* + past participle. We use past perfect for actions that happened earlier in the past.

• *I couldn't get on the plane because I had left my passport at home* (= I left my passport at home, then I couldn't get on the plane).

Compare past perfect and past simple:

• *When I arrived, Mark left*
(= I arrived and then Mark left).
• *When I arrived, Mark had left*
(= Mark left before I arrived).

Reported speech

direct speech	reported speech
present simple	past simple
present continuous	past continuous
past simple	past perfect
present perfect	past perfect
past perfect	past perfect
am / is / are going to	was / were going to
will	would
can	could

In reported speech the tense moves one back.

• *'I like action films.'* → *He said (that) he liked action films.*
• *'I told Sam about the party.'* → *He said (that) he had told Sam about the party.*

direct speech	reported speech
today	that day
tomorrow	the following day
yesterday	the day before

Time expressions also change in reported speech.

• *'I will do it tomorrow.'* → *She said (that) she would do it the following day.*
• *'I saw her yesterday.'* → *He said (that) he had seen her the day before.*

Reported questions

In reported questions, we use the same tense changes as in reported speech.

The word order in reported questions also changes.

• *'Where is your house?'* → *He asked me where my house was.*
  NOT *He asked me where is my house.*
• *'How old are you?'* → *She asked me how old I was.*

In reported *yes / no* questions, we use *if*.

• *'Do you enjoy your job?'* → *He asked me if I enjoyed my job.*
  NOT *He asked me did I enjoy my job.*
• *'Have you met Tim?'* → *She asked me if I had met Tim.*

PET Transcripts

Unit 1

Lesson 1, Activities 2 and 3

COREY: Hi, I'm Corey.

MIKI: Hi, I'm Miki, nice to meet you. Where are you from Corey?

COREY: I'm from Canada. I've just moved here.

MIKI: Canada! Are you good at winter sports then?

COREY: Well I love playing ice hockey. And in summer I enjoy tennis and mountain biking.

MIKI: Wow! That's quite dangerous isn't it.

COREY: Not really. Not if you're careful. What do you do in your free time?

MIKI: I quite like playing tennis too, and I love playing football. But I'm also very interested in acting and I really love the theatre – I want to be an actress one day. Have you got any other hobbies?

COREY: Um, I guess I enjoy playing online computer games and meeting new people there. How about you? Do you spend much time online?

MIKI: Well I'm not keen on computer games. But I've got a MySpace page and I like chatting online there or on other social websites. But I really prefer chatting face to face with my friends. Especially at weekends.

COREY: What kind of things do you do with them?

MIKI: We love going shopping, even if we don't buy anything.

COREY: Really? I hate it! Although I suppose I don't mind music stores. I really like dance music. What kind of music do you like?

MIKI: Pop mostly – but you should have a look at my MySpace page sometime – just search for Mikaela.

COREY: Is that M I C H A E L A?

MIKI: No, M I K A E L A.

COREY: OK, I will. Mine's Coldfield.

MIKI: How do you spell that?

COREY: C O L D F I E L D

MIKI: Great, I'll check it out. Anyway it's time for registration – and after that I'll introduce you to some of my friends.

Unit 2

Lesson 1, Activities 2 and 3

I've got two brothers, and we're all pretty creative. My older brother Steve is the most hard-working of us three brothers. He's a producer and makes documentary films for television. It sounds exciting, but he works until very late at night, and is always tired. I'm a musician and I sometimes write background music for Steve's films. I love it, I've got the best job in the world. Steve and I both went to university but I didn't spend as much time studying as he did. I was always too busy playing in my band. Tim's the youngest in the family, though he's actually taller than either Steve or me. And we're certainly not as good-looking as he is. He was the most popular boy in the school. He never seemed to work very hard but he's not as lazy as I was. He's at art college now, and works as a waiter in his spare time. He's an absolutely brilliant artist and his drawings are really amazing. I think he'll be more successful than either of us in the future.

Lesson 2, Activity 7

1

I really liked our apartment in the city centre, but Dad found living there too noisy so we moved here. He loves the beautiful views and the peace and quiet, but I have a long bus journey to school every day and I miss my friends. Mum's seen a nice house in town that would be much more convenient and I could still have my own room. I know the garden's not as big as this one but it's much bigger than the balcony we had in the apartment.

2

GIRL: Shall we go clubbing on Saturday night?

BOY: I can't. I have to write an essay on Sunday – and anyway, I haven't got much money. Why don't you come round and watch a DVD with a pizza or something?

GIRL: Oh, come on! Your sister will be back from university for the weekend. She'll want to go clubbing.

BOY: Yeah, OK. I'm sure she'll lend me some money. I'll try and finish my essay tonight.

3

GIRL: I like that computer desk Tom. Is it new?

BOY: Yeah. I wanted something a bit more modern. You know, metal legs, a glass top and shelves on top, but Mum thought it might get broken. She wanted me to get a plain wooden one. I saw a really nice one, but it only had one drawer and I need at least three for all my stuff. Anyway, we were just leaving when I saw this one – I know it's painted but it's got the right number of drawers and I like the light colour.

4

GIRL: Hey, what about this poster. That's your favourite band, right?

BOY: They were, but I'm not so keen on them any more. This one's better – Lewis Hamilton winning the Formula One championship.

GIRL: Really? Cars are so boring! Wow! Look at these whales! They're great, and at least this poster would be relaxing.

BOY: Hm. I'd rather have a picture of someone I really admire. It makes me want to succeed too.

Unit 3

Lesson 1, Activity 4

CARL: Hi Jennie. Have you written your essay yet?

JENNIE: The one about life being better 100 years ago? Not yet. I can't decide what to write.

CARL: Really? I finished my essay last night. No cars, no electricity, no central heating, no television. It's obvious life was much worse.

JENNIE: Yes, but I think there were still some good points. Food for example. There were no ready meals or fast food, so people grew their own fruit and vegetables. Surely that was better for them than a lot of what we eat today?

CARL: Well, maybe, but did everybody use to eat like that? I don't think so. And what about clothes? Did you know that boys used to wear dresses and have long hair until they were about five years old? How embarrassing!

JENNIE: I know, but I find that funny. And there were some beautiful clothes for women. Anyway, you said there was no television. That meant people made music or performed plays in the evenings. That has to be better than sitting in front of the box.

CARL: Well I'd rather watch TV than play the piano.

JENNIE: I think it's a great skill to have. And I definitely think children had more respect for adults a hundred years ago.

CARL: True. But that was because the kids were afraid of being punished - and we'd find some of those punishments quite cruel nowadays. Not to mention all the terrible diseases and the fog because of the coal fires and the hard work - I could go on and on ...

JENNIE: Oh yes, I know. Can you imagine - the poor housewife used to clean the house and wash the clothes by hand every week. People didn't have washing machines or vacuum cleaners. That's why they needed servants.

CARL: Aren't you glad you live in the 21st century?

JENNIE: Yes, I suppose I am. OK, well, thanks Carl - you've given me some useful ideas. Now all I need to do is write them up as an essay!

Lesson 1, Activities 8 and 9

DIMITRI: What sort of things do you do with your family Elena?

ELENA: Well, I'm a college student now so I live with friends and don't spend so much time at home. But I always have dinner with my family on a Sunday, sometimes at home or sometimes in a restaurant. What about you Dimitri?

DIMITRI: I live at home so my family eat together every day. And I play football with my brothers, and I go to football matches with my dad at weekends. Erm ... Do you go on holiday with your family?

ELENA: I used to. It was fun when I was little and we all did things together but now everyone wants different things. Now I prefer to go with my friends.

DIMITRI: That's interesting. It's the same for me. We don't go on holiday as a family now. I think it's much more fun with friends!

ELENA: Me too, definitely!

DIMITRI: What else...? My parents used to help me with my homework when I was younger - with things like Maths and Science.

ELENA: You were lucky. I had to do my homework on my own. And I couldn't watch television until I'd finished.

DIMITRI: Wow! I would hate that! Did you also have to help your parents in the house?

ELENA: Just little things like laying the table and doing the washing up. What about you?

DIMITRI: Sometimes my parents gave me extra pocket money if I helped them with the housework - did the shopping or washed the dishes maybe. But now I just do my own things. I make my bed and sometimes clean my room.

ELENA: Really? I have to do all my own housework - there are lots of advantages to living at home!

Unit 4

Lesson 1, Activity 3

1

STEVEN: What kind of food shall I have at my party, Mum?

MUM: Well, I'm not sure. What about pizza?

STEVEN: Again? I had that last year! Can't you make your special fried chicken?

MUM: What a good idea! And why don't we make a big green salad to go with it?

2

SISTER: It's Mum and Dad's wedding anniversary next month, isn't it? Shall we organise a party for them?

BROTHER: Oh, I don't think that's a good idea. Dad hates parties. And anyway, I haven't got time. I need to study for my exams.

SISTER: Hm. You're right. It's too much work. Let's just take them out to a restaurant.

BROTHER: Yes, that's the best idea. We should book it soon!

3

GIRL: Have you bought anything for Pablo's birthday yet?

BOY: No, not yet. I might get him a computer game.

GIRL: That's not a bad idea. But they're pretty expensive.

BOY: I know, why don't we buy him one together?

GIRL: Great idea! Do you think he would like *Empire Battles*?

BOY: Probably, but he could already have that one. I think we should ask his brother which one he wants.

GIRL: OK.

Lesson 1, Activity 6

SISTER: It's Mum and Dad's wedding anniversary next month, isn't it? Shall we organise a party for them?

BROTHER: Oh, I don't think that's a good idea. Dad hates parties. And anyway, I haven't got time. I need to study for my exams.

SISTER: Hm. You're right. It's too much work. Let's just take them out to a restaurant.

BROTHER: Yes, that's the best idea. We should book it soon!

Lesson 1, Activity 9

GIRL: What do you think about this idea - going for a picnic?

BOY: Well, I'm not sure. I think it's a bit boring. I think a barbecue on the beach would be more fun.

GIRL: Yes, I agree, but it's quite a lot of work. Someone has to stand there and cook all night. And it might rain! I think they should go to a restaurant instead. They could have a really nice meal, roast chicken, steak …

BOY: That's true, but it's quite expensive to go to a restaurant. Some people may not have enough money.

GIRL: Well, what about having a DVD party at someone's house? They could order a pizza or just have some snacks. That wouldn't be expensive and it would be easy for everyone. They could throw all the rubbish away afterwards, so there's no washing up!

BOY: I suppose so. But it's not very exciting, is it? I think a fancy dress party is a good idea. They could have a competition and decide who is wearing the best costume. And for food, everyone could bring a different dish. That way they can share the work.

GIRL: Yes, you're right. I think that's the best idea too.

Lesson 2, Activities 2 and 4

KATH: Hi Vanessa. Did you have a good time at *Charlie's* last night?

VANESSA: Oh hi, Kath. No, it was terrible! I'm never going to that restaurant again!

KATH: Really? I'm surprised! I went there several times last year, and I always had a lot of fun. I saw a couple of famous people there last time!

VANESSA: Yeah, I know. I thought it was going to be really stylish and fashionable, but I was so disappointed! We were the only people there. Can you believe it? There was no atmosphere at all.

KATH: And what about the food?

VANESSA: Well, the soup was too salty and the chocolate dessert was bitter. And the fish was covered in a really horrible sauce.

KATH: Oh dear!

VANESSA: Yeah, it was disgusting! And the service was terrible too. There were plenty of waiters but none of them wanted to serve us. They were really unfriendly and the food took hours to arrive.

KATH: Oh dear. Plenty of things to complain about then?

VANESSA: Yeah, I talked to the manager before we left, but he didn't seem to care at all.

Unit 5
Lesson 1, Activity 4

1

More problems for star tennis player Justin Brown, who only returned to first class tennis a few weeks ago. He was absent from the game for several months last year because of an operation on his arm. In today's match against Fernando Garcia of Spain he slipped and fell heavily on the grass court, hurting his ankle. He was taken straight to hospital for X-rays. Doctors say the injury is not serious and fortunately there is no damage to his knee.

2

PATIENT: So, what can I do so that my shoulder gets better quickly?

DOCTOR: Well, some exercise will definitely help. Swimming is very good because the water supports your arms. But playing the violin has caused your problem so you should avoid that for at least a fortnight. You really ought to stop practising for a while.

PATIENT: Right, I'll do that. What about using the computer?

DOCTOR: That's OK, but you should make sure you take a break every half hour.

3

GIRL 1: What's the matter, Rosie? I thought you were going to the hairdresser's today.

GIRL 2: I've put it off until next week. I've had earache and toothache all day so I saw the college doctor at lunchtime. He said my ear was OK but he gave me some painkillers and said I ought to see my dentist as soon as possible. His earliest appointment is tomorrow morning.

GIRL 1: Poor you. How are you feeling now?

GIRL 2: Not great. Earache's bad enough but toothache's even worse!

4

WOMAN: How was your holiday - no accidents this year I hope?

MAN: Well, actually Molly hurt her finger playing tennis and had to have it X-rayed. Fortunately it wasn't broken, but she had a big bandage on it for the rest of the holiday. At least it wasn't as bad as last year when Tom fell off his bike and broke his arm.

WOMAN: You are unlucky! The worst problem we've ever had on holiday is insect bites.

MAN: Ah well, we still had a great time. That's the main thing.

Unit 6

Lesson 2, Activity 4

INTERVIEWER: Good evening and welcome to *Our World*. Tonight's guest is the explorer Sally Brendle. Sally, you've been on expeditions to some of the most unspoilt forests on the planet. What is it like?

SALLY: Fantastic. There's nothing better than being the first scientist to see a particular river, for example, or to find a new plant or animal. On my most recent trip, we were looking for a rare crocodile in a rainforest in Asia but we discovered a previously unknown snake. Although it was tiny and completely harmless, it was still very exciting.

INTERVIEWER: It sounds it! So, tell us about your early life. How did you become an explorer?

SALLY: Well, I've been interested in nature ever since I was a young child. While my friends were playing games, I used to go fishing or looking for animals in the fields near my home. I wasn't interested in *protecting* creatures in those days. In fact, I used to catch them to put them in my own little zoo!

INTERVIEWER: And what was your first expedition?

SALLY: As soon as I was eighteen, I went to Africa, with an organisation called Africa Exchange. They run different projects. Things like helping to build schools or studying how monkeys behave. My job was to count how many lions and elephants there were in a certain area every day. That was a fantastic introduction, and really important for the protection programme.

INTERVIEWER: And what did you do after that?

SALLY: While I was at university I met a famous Brazilian explorer. He was planning an expedition to the Amazon rainforest in order to study the plants that people use for medicine. A team member broke her leg so he asked me to go in her place.

INTERVIEWER: Can you describe what it's like to be in a rainforest?

SALLY: Well, the thing I always notice is the atmosphere. Although it's not silent, the noises are all natural, which I find very relaxing. Despite the heat and the wildlife, it's quite safe if you're careful. Modern technology means you can't really get lost nowadays.

INTERVIEWER: Mm. And finally, Sally, would you like to tell us a bit about your new TV series?

SALLY: Yes, of course. It's called *Secrets of the Rainforest*. Of course, it's no secret that many animals will disappear unless they are protected. The idea is to show people that it's not just popular animals like tigers that are in danger. There are lots of animals in the world's rainforests that no one has heard of and many of them need our help too. So in this programme we introduce people to some of those.

INTERVIEWER: Well, it sounds really interesting. I can't wait to see it!

Unit 7

Lesson 1, Activities 2 and 3

INTERVIEWER: Thanks for making time to talk to us, Kirsty. Perhaps you could start by telling us about a typical day's training.

KIRSTY: Sure. Well, Tuesday's my busiest day. I get up at around eight and pack my bag. There's a lot of equipment when you do five different sports! Then I drive to the sports village for 9.30. I spend an hour at the training centre doing target practice. I must admit, shooting's the sport I enjoy the least. Then I go swimming. It's only a short walk to the pool. I swim 3,500 metres, though I could easily swim further in an hour and a half. At midday I have lunch and discuss my progress with my coaches.

INTERVIEWER: I guess there's lots to talk about.

KIRSTY: Yeah, but I can't spend too long with them because I go riding at half past one. I put on my riding clothes, apart from my boots and helmet, before I leave for the riding school - it's about half an hour away. There are several horses that I ride. Some of them go better than others, but they're all pretty good.

INTERVIEWER: Do you ride all afternoon?

KIRSTY: I'd like to but I go fencing at three. I'm afraid I often drive faster than I should to get back in time for my lesson. I change into my fencing uniform and put on the special glove and helmet. The lesson is only 20 minutes but fencing's the sport where I have to work the hardest.

INTERVIEWER: Can you relax a bit after that?

KIRSTY: Not exactly - I put on my shorts and running shoes for a gentle run around the track with some of the other athletes. It's not a race so it doesn't matter if I run more slowly than they do. Afterwards I go home for a meal and a short rest.

INTERVIEWER: You must be ready for that. How do you spend your evenings?

KIRSTY: At 6.30 I come back to the sports centre and play football for an hour. This is the activity I enjoy the most. My day finishes after I've done some exercises in the gym. At 9 p.m. I can go home and have a rest or, more likely, get ready for the next day.

INTERVIEWER: Well just listening to you makes me feel tired. Now, how about your plans for ...

Lesson 2, Activity 6

Are you a fan of the crime writer, Jacquie Cooper? Have you ever dreamed of seeing your artwork on the front of a book?

To celebrate Jacquie Cooper's fiftieth birthday this year, we have organised a competition. Listeners are invited to design a cover for a special edition of Jacquie's best-selling novel, *Midnight*. It's a thriller about a young man who accidentally joins a group of criminals after an evening out with his friends.

The competition will be judged by Jacquie herself and Suzie Wilson. Suzie, who is probably best known for presenting the popular music show, *Concert Club*, is also Jacquie's daughter and a keen collector of art.

You can design your book cover on the computer, or by hand, with pen and ink or pencil. However, you should not use paint in this competition. Your work should be 20 centimetres by 13 centimetres in size and the design should include the title, the author's name and somewhere on the cover, a small dog, which Jacquie's publishers will use in their advertisements. The rest is up to you, so be imaginative!

The prize-winning design will appear on the book cover and, in addition, the winner will meet Jacquie and go to lunch with her at a top London restaurant. The five second prize winners will each receive a signed copy of one of Jacquie's books.

We must receive your entry by post or email no later than the 30th April – that's a Wednesday. We will contact the winners on May the 28th and their names will be announced on this programme on May the 30th. Make a note of those dates so you don't miss them.

You'll find further details of this competition and some useful tips on our website at www …

Unit 8

Lesson 2, Activity 4

Hello everyone. My name's Sandy Duffy and I'm here to tell you about my career as a video game writer. I work with game developers and designers to think of good stories, and I write all the dialogue in the game. When I was in secondary school, I never imagined that I would do this job! I played the violin and that's what I planned to do as my job. But I had an accident when I was playing basketball and hurt my hand, so I had to think of another career. My mother wanted me to be a journalist, but I didn't think it was for me.

I didn't know what to study at university. I was good at lots of science subjects, including Physics and Maths, but I also loved entertaining people and I was good at Art. In the end I went to film school where I studied lighting, special effects, how to use a camera … all that! It was there that I started to think about working in the video game industry.

Now, a question that everyone always asks me is, 'How did you get your first job?' Well, I had a friend whose job was organising conferences. At one of the conferences, she met a man who owned a company that made video games. I wrote to him and sent my CV. He obviously liked what he read because he gave me an interview and offered me a job as a junior.

People also ask me what I like best about being a video game writer. Well, the money is good and it's quite exciting. Just last night, for example, I was at a big dinner where they were giving prizes for new games. But what I love is the fact that I get on so well with everyone in the business. That's what makes my job so much fun.

Obviously no job is perfect, though, and there are things I don't like. I've just started a new job, and I have to spend a lot of time on the road or at the airport, which I find very hard. I'd really like to be able to spend more time at home.

So, what should you do if you want to be a video game writer? Well, there are people who say you can do it without going to university, but I don't think that's true any more. In my opinion you should work hard at school and get a good degree. And read lots of books – that will help you later when you need to think up stories for new games!

Unit 9

Lesson 2, Activity 4

Now, I want to tell you about a fantastic new exhibition at the Science Museum. It's called 'A Changing World' and is all about global warming. It opens to the public on the 23rd of August and runs until December the 16th.

The first thing you'll notice when you walk in is hundreds of pairs of Wellington boots. Everyone needs to put on a pair of these because the whole exhibition area is flooded with water. The idea is to show what will happen if sea levels continue to rise. It really makes you think!

One of the best displays is the one about the Arctic. In this room there is a huge block of ice, which is slowly melting. There are also a number of photographs, which show really clearly how the sea ice is disappearing year after year.

As you walk around the exhibition, you'll see that all over the walls there are posters which explain the causes and effects of global warming. The content was written especially for this exhibition by a number of well-known scientists, so you can be sure you are getting the most up-to-date information possible.

In the film room you can see several short films which tell some personal stories about the effects of global warming. There are people from Greenland, Australia, Canada and Brazil. Some of the stories are quite shocking.

At the end of the exhibition there are some computers. You can use these to send emails, either to politicians, telling them what you want them to do, or to a friend. You can let them know what you have learned or give them some advice on what they can do to stop global warming.

It's one of the best exhibitions about global warming that I've ever seen and I recommend it to everyone!

Unit 10

Lesson 1, Activity 2

SHONA: Jim, we've really got to sort out our holiday before everything gets booked up. Why don't we go to that hotel in the mountains we went to last year? That was great, wasn't it?

JIM: Yeah, but would we enjoy it as much if we went there again? I think we should do something else this year.

SHONA: OK, I suppose you're right. Have you got any ideas then?

JIM: Yes, I have actually. Remember that TV programme we saw about the Arctic Circle? I'd love to go there. We could do a cruise and see all that amazing scenery on the coast.

SHONA: Yes, but I remember they said the weather could be terrible. If it rained all the time we wouldn't see the scenery. And you know I always get seasick on boats.

JIM: Oh yeah, I forgot. That wouldn't be much fun. Well, what about a beach holiday for a change?

SHONA: Come on! You know we'd be bored if we spent a week lying on the beach.

JIM: Well, yes of course we would. But we're both good swimmers. Why don't we use the opportunity to try something new like windsurfing or sailing?

SHONA: Yes, or diving! If we learned to dive we could explore underwater and see some fantastic fish.

JIM: The problem is, we'd have to do a course and a written test. I don't want to spend my holiday studying.

SHONA: OK, well why don't you do windsurfing or sailing and I'll learn to dive. That way we'll both be happy.

JIM: Brilliant. Now we just need to decide where to go. Let's get some brochures. If we go now the travel agent's will still be open.

SHONA: No need. We can just look on the internet. There's more choice, and we can book it straight away.

JIM: OK, let's have a look.

Unit 11

Lesson 1, Activity 3

1

BOY: Hang on, here's the music store. Let's go in! I want to listen to some of the new CDs.

GIRL: Why don't you buy your trainers first? The sports shop's just next door. We can meet back here in half an hour.

BOY: Aren't you going to help me choose some trainers?

GIRL: No way! There are some great dresses in that clothes shop over there. I want to try some on.

BOY: OK. See you later.

2

Welcome to ShopRight. We have some extra special offers for you today. On the first floor there's a fifty percent discount on jeans for women. Take the lift to the second floor for our special menswear offers. Buy one of our exciting new stripy woollen jumpers together with a striped cotton shirt and we'll give you a smart leather belt at no extra cost. If you're hungry, why not try the special lunch in the third floor café – soup, salad and a drink all for only five pounds.

3

FRIEND: Did you buy anything in town yesterday, Donna?

DONNA: Yes, I bought this amazing red leather bag and a fantastic new skirt.

FRIEND: Ooh, is that it? It's a lovely blue colour!

DONNA: I've had this one for months. I actually saw two that I loved. I tried on a beautiful green silk skirt and a bright yellow one like yours. They were both great but the yellow one didn't fit so I got the other one. I'll wear it tomorrow to show you.

4

FRIEND: Hey Danny. Where are you going?

DANNY: Into town. I've finally saved up enough money for that new computer game, *Heroes of the Earth*. Do you want to come with me?

FRIEND: Sure, but it's cheaper online you know.

DANNY: Yeah, I know. It's just like ordering by phone. You get it a bit cheaper, but you've got to wait ages for it to arrive in the post. I want to be able to play it straight away.

FRIEND: And it's fun trying out all the other games in the shop. OK. Let's go then.

Lesson 2, Activities 7 and 8

Welcome to the Golden Court Shopping Centre. We'll be here until 4 p.m. this afternoon. It's the biggest shopping centre in the country and there are hundreds of shops selling everything you could possibly want. I'm just going to tell you a little bit about the facilities and services that are available here.

If you need to change foreign money there is a bank on the first floor, but you can use a card to get money from any of the cash machines on the ground floor.

For those of you who don't want to spend all day shopping, the cinema is on the second floor and is showing twelve different films today. If you want to see a film please make sure it finishes before 3.30 p.m. because we must be on the bus by five to four.

If you want a special souvenir to remember the trip by, why not have your picture painted? There are always several artists in the area around the main entrance. For a head and shoulders painting, expect to pay around £25 and allow an hour and a half.

Some of you may want to call your parents, but I should warn you that it will cost a lot if you use the pay phone in the shopping centre. It's much cheaper to go to the internet café and ask to use their special service.

For lunch, there are several restaurants and cafés on the third floor. If you like Italian food, Pronto Pizzas will give you a discount if you show your Travel Tours badge.

If anybody gets lost or needs to see me, you can return here to the information desk. The assistant will contact me, and I'll come and find you.

OK, I think that's everything. Have fun and I'll see you all later!

Unit 12

Lesson 1, Activity 5

INTERVIEWER: James, you've had a very successful career as a film director. But tell me, can you remember the very first time you went to the cinema?

JAMES: Oh yes, very clearly! It was a Saturday morning in 1937 and my parents were chatting over breakfast about how they'd spent the previous evening. They were talking about 'the pictures'. That's what we used to call films in those days. I was fascinated. I was about five years old and, until that day, I had never seen a film. I hadn't even heard of television - in fact we didn't even have a telephone in our house. Our only contact with the outside world came from the radio in the sitting room.

I started pleading with my father to take me to see a film. I think he felt a bit guilty because they'd left me with a babysitter the night before. Anyway, whatever the reason, he took me to the cinema that very afternoon.

The size of it amazed me, and I loved the atmosphere immediately. In those days there was still an usherette - a girl who showed you to your seats in the dark if you arrived after the film had started - and she was there with her tray of sweets and ice cream in the breaks. My mother had given me some money before we left home, so I queued up and bought myself some chocolates. I remember I felt very grown up!

But the film itself was the most important thing. When the curtains opened and the lights went down, I couldn't believe my eyes. There was the screen, with huge close-ups of the characters. There were sudden changes of scene that took my breath away, and action that was shown from many different angles. Obviously audiences are used to all that now - these days film scenes only last a few seconds and are filled with special effects. In those days one scene could last for several minutes. And of course the sets were very basic, if you compare them to today's.

But the performances the actors gave were wonderful. I had never experienced anything like it and I loved the cinema from that point on. And, no, I can't remember what the film was called!

Exam Guide

Listening Part 1

WOMAN: Oh no! I haven't got my mobile!

MAN: But you used it just now to book a table at the restaurant.

WOMAN: Oh, I remember. I put it down on the steps while I put my coat on.

MAN: Well, let's walk back quickly - it might still be there.

1

MALE: I'm really looking forward to the concert tomorrow! It starts at three, doesn't it? Shall I meet you there at about ten to?

FEMALE: Well, I don't like the first band, so I'm not planning to get there until four.

MALE: OK. I'll see you then near the entrance.

FEMALE: Fine, don't forget your mobile in case I can't see you.

2

Good afternoon everyone and welcome to today's talk. Our speaker this evening is William Long, the author of *A long way up*. He is going to tell us all about his latest adventure - a balloon flight over the Sahara desert. He will also talk about past successes, such as his journey into the heart of the African jungle and his diving expedition off the coast of India. These are truly amazing stories and I do hope you enjoy listening to them.

3

RACHEL: How was your holiday Steve? Did you do lots of fun sports?

STEVE: Kind of. We had great weather. It was sunny and warm but unfortunately there wasn't enough wind to go sailing. That made it perfect for cycling though. I hadn't done it for ages and I really enjoyed it.

RACHEL: That's good. Did you get to go surfing at all?

STEVE: Unfortunately not - no wind means no waves. But we still had a great time.

4

MUM: What time are you supposed to be at the cinema Tony? It's seven o'clock you know!

TONY: On no, is it? I'm meeting Philip at seven fifteen. I was going to walk, but I don't think I've got enough time now. Maybe if I run for the bus, I'll just get there in time.

MUM: Only if the bus comes straight away, and it never does. Come on, I'll give you a lift. I need to get a few things from the supermarket anyway.

TONY: Great, thanks Mum.

5

Hello, this is a message for Fiona Green. I'm calling about your appointment with the dentist on Friday the 15th of June. I'm sorry but I've had to cancel that appointment as the dentist will now be away between the 15th and 19th of June. He can see you at quarter past four on the 22nd of June or, if that isn't convenient, call me at 9 a.m. on the 20th of June and we can arrange another day.

6

FIONA: Luke, have you bought a present for Karen yet? It's her birthday party on Saturday, isn't it?

LUKE: Yes, but I still don't know what to get her. Jim's bought her that DVD she wanted, and I can't think of anything else.

FIONA: She loves jewellery. Do you want me to come shopping with you tomorrow? I could help you choose something. Or you could get her a book – she likes reading.

LUKE: That's a bit boring. I like your first idea best. I'll pick you up at ten o'clock tomorrow!

7

MAN: What would you like to drink? Coffee? Or do you feel like a cold drink?

WOMAN: I think I'll have a lemonade. I've had two cups of coffee already today. And can I have a piece of that chocolate cake? It looks really good.

MAN: OK. I'll have some too, with a cup of coffee. You go and find us a table and I'll queue up to buy it.

WOMAN: OK. Thanks.

Listening Part 2

INTERVIEWER: Welcome, Joe Durrant. You made an amazing journey, travelling 3,000 kilometres across Europe on a skateboard. What made you decide to do it?

JOE: Two years ago I was feeling bored with my job and was looking for a challenge. I heard about an organisation called Boardwalk that helps teenagers with difficulties. I'm good at skateboarding and I know Europe well, so I thought, why not raise money for Boardwalk by skateboarding through France to the Spanish capital Madrid – about 3,000 kilometres.

INTERVIEWER: Did you get help from local businesses?

JOE: Definitely. I already had all the camping equipment I needed, so several firms gave money to Boardwalk instead. And I'd organised several trips across Europe as a student so deciding which route to take wasn't a problem. The travel agent in my town provided boat tickets to our starting point on the north coast of France, which was great.

INTERVIEWER: Yes! Did you travel on your own?

JOE: Two friends in their camper van acted as a back-up vehicle. They didn't actually follow me but they carried the tents and luggage between the overnight stops, and we met up at the end of each day. Funnily enough, their van broke down a couple of times, while I had no problems at all with my skateboard, although I took several spare sets of wheels.

INTERVIEWER: But how many pairs of shoes did you need?

JOE: Five pairs! There was one pair of trainers that only lasted a day. That was crossing the mountains into Spain. The roads were really steep and stony and I could see snow up on the mountain tops. Coming down was terrible because I had to use my foot as a brake. By the end of the day, the new pair of trainers I'd put on that morning were ruined and I had to throw them away.

INTERVIEWER: Oh no! Did you have any accidents?

JOE: Just one, in Barcelona. And I wasn't even on my skateboard! I was having my photo taken for my website. I jumped up and landed on a piece of metal and cut my foot. I couldn't walk for ten days afterwards but I was more worried about my camera, which I'd dropped as I fell. Luckily it wasn't damaged.

INTERVIEWER: And how do you feel now it's all over?

JOE: Fantastic because it has been so successful for Boardwalk. I'd love to work for them one day. I expected to feel depressed but I've been busy writing a book about my trip. It isn't always easy but it's good fun!

INTERVIEWER: That's great. Thanks for talking to us, Joe.

Listening Part 3

Superstars Drama School is offering two fantastic courses this summer. One is called Musical Theatre and the other is Comedy Acting – especially for those of you who are good at making people laugh. Our Screen Acting class, which is always popular, will return in the autumn.

All of our teachers are professional actors who will give you individual attention and the best advice possible. Each course is 30 hours per week and runs for three weeks. If you book within the next two weeks you'll get a ten percent discount.

Our school offers top quality facilities. We have several comfortable classrooms and a video recording studio. The garden is perfect for relaxing in, and we have a student café where hot and cold drinks, as well as sandwiches, are available. If you prefer a hot meal at lunchtime there are restaurants nearby.

The school is easy to get to using public transport. Two buses stop outside the school, the number sixty-two and the three-eight-one. Heyburn train station is a twenty-minute walk away or a short bus ride. It's best to leave your car at home as there is no parking at the school.

For visitors who need it, we can offer accommodation in our student hostel which is just a fifteen-minute walk from the school. It's in a lovely area with lots of great shops nearby. Many of them stay open until quite late. Bedrooms are single or shared. Pillows and duvets are provided, but students are asked to bring their own sheets. There's a modern kitchen with everything you need to prepare your meals. The housekeeper, Mrs Russell, is a great favourite with the students there and will make sure you have a happy stay.

Have a look at our website, www.superstars.co.uk, for more information and an online booking form.

Listening Part 4

STEVE: Hi Claire. You look a bit depressed. What's the matter?

CLAIRE: Hi Steve. Well, it's my dad. I'm really annoyed with him. I hate it when we get cross with each other but you'll never believe what he's done.

STEVE: Well go on, tell me. What has he done?

CLAIRE: Well you know my mum is always telling me to tidy my bedroom? Dad's only gone and posted a picture of my untidy room on his website. I'm so embarrassed. I'm twenty and I've got a job and he's acting as if I'm still a little kid.

STEVE: I suppose he wants to make you feel ashamed so that you clean it up. Have you tidied it up now?

CLAIRE: Not yet. I'm not going to let him think his plan has been successful. Anyway it's impossible to keep my room tidy all the time because it's so small. I clean it every Sunday morning but by the following Saturday it's always very untidy.

STEVE: Well I wouldn't worry too much about the picture online. I'm sure that he just meant it as a joke. And how many people do you think will look at your dad's website and recognise your room?

CLAIRE: I hadn't thought of that – not many I'm sure.

STEVE: Well there you are. But have you thought about finding somewhere else to live?

CLAIRE: Of course, but everywhere is so expensive.

STEVE: You know that my sister's been looking for a new apartment. She's found one that she really likes but it's too big for one person so she's going to try to find a flatmate.

CLAIRE: Really? That sounds perfect. What's your sister like?

STEVE: Very relaxed and easy going – I'm sure you'd get on well together.

CLAIRE: And I'm sure I would be much tidier if I had more space.

STEVE: Well here's her number, anyway.

CLAIRE: Thanks Steve, I'll get in touch with her right away!

PET Vocabulary list

Unit 1

hobbies and interests

acting	n	/'æktɪŋ/
athletics	n	/æθ'letɪks/)
chatting online	n	/'tʃætɪŋ ɒnlaɪn/
fashion	n	/'fæʃən/
football (AmE soccer)	n	/'fʊtbɔːl/ (AmE /'sɒkər/)
going to the gym	n	/'ɡəʊɪŋ tə ðə 'dʒɪm/
hockey	n	/'hɒki/)
keeping fit	n	/kiːpɪŋ 'fɪt/
making new friends	n	/'meɪkɪŋ njuː 'frendz/
meeting new people	n	/'miːtɪŋ njuː 'piːpl/
mountain biking	n	/'maʊntɪn 'baɪkɪŋ/
music	n	/'mjuːzɪk/
playing online computer games	n	/'pleɪɪŋ 'ɒnlaɪn kəm'pjuːtə geɪmz/ (AmE /'pleɪɪŋ 'ɒnlaɪn kəm'pjuːtər geɪmz/)
shopping	n	/'ʃɒpɪŋ/
tennis	n	/'tenɪs/
volleyball	n	/'vɒlibɔːl/

communication and technology

email	n	/'iːmeɪl/
internet	n	/'ɪntənet/ (AmE /'ɪntərnet/)
landline	n	/'lændlaɪn/
laptop	n	/'læptɒp/
mobile phone	n	/'məʊbaɪl fəʊn/
postcard	n	/'pəʊstkɑːd/ (AmE /'pəʊstkɑːrd/)
social network	n	/'səʊʃəl 'netwɜːk/ (AmE /'səʊʃəl 'netwɜːrk/)
text message	n	/'tekst mesɪdʒ/
web page	n	/'web peɪdʒ/
website	n	/'websaɪt/

communication and technology verbs

click	v	/klɪk/
communicate	v	/kəm'juːnikeɪt/
crash	v	/kræʃ/
delete	v	/dɪ'liːt/
keep in touch	v	/kiːp ɪn 'tʌtʃ/
save	v	/seɪv/
surf	v	/sɜːf/ (AmE /sɜːrf/)
switch off	v	/swɪtʃ ɒf/
text	v	/tekst/

Unit 2

family

elderly	adj	/'eldəli/ (AmE /'eldərli/)
grandparent	n	/'grænpeərənt/
in his / her thirties	phr	/ɪn hɪz / hə 'θɜːtiz/ (AmE /ɪn hɪz / hər 'θɜːrtiz/)
in his / her twenties	phr	/ɪn hɪz / hə 'twentiz/ (AmE /ɪn hɪz / hər 'twentiz/)
teenager	n	/'tiːneɪdʒə/ (AmE /'tiːneɪdʒər/)
twins	n	/twɪnz/

adjectives for describing people

attractive	adj	/ə'træktɪv/
bald	adj	/bɔːld/
handsome	adj	/'hænsəm/

pretty	adj	/'prɪti/
slim	adj	/slɪm/
tall	adj	/tɔːl/

nouns for describing people

beard	n	/bɪəd/ (AmE /bɪərd/)
blonde hair	n	/'blɒnd heə/ (AmE /'blɒnd heər/)
curly hair	n	/'kɜːli heə/ (AmE /'kɜːrli heər/)
dark hair	n	/'dɑːk heə/ (AmE /'dɑːrk heər/)
fair hair	n	/'feə heə/ (AmE /'feər heər/)
glasses	n	/'glɑːsɪz/ (AmE /'glæsɪz/)
moustache	n	/məs'tɑːʃ/ (AmE /'mʌstæʃ/)

character

cheerful	adj	/'tʃɪəfʊl/ (AmE /'tʃɪrfʊl/)
confident	adj	/'kɒnfɪdənt/
hard-working	adj	/'hɑːd wɜːkɪŋ/ (AmE /'hɑːrd wɜːrkɪŋ/)
kind	adj	/kaɪnd/
lazy	adj	/'leɪzi/
lonely	adj	/'ləʊnli/
rude	adj	/ruːd/
shy	adj	/ʃaɪ/
unkind	adj	/ʌn'kaɪnd/

extreme adjectives

amazing	adj	/ə'meɪzɪŋ/
awful	adj	/'ɔːfəl/
brilliant	adj	/'brɪljənt/

furniture and furnishings

armchair	n	/'ɑːmtʃeə/ (AmE /'ɑːrmtʃeər/)
blinds	n	/blaɪndz/
carpet	n	/'kɑːpɪt/ (AmE /'kɑːrpɪt/)
ceiling	n	/'siːlɪŋ/
cupboard	n	/'kʌbəd/ (AmE /'kʌbərd/)
curtains	n	/'kɜːtənz/ (AmE /'kɜːrtənz/)
cushion	n	/'kʊʃən/
desk	n	/desk/
drawers	n	/drɔːz/ (AmE /drɔːrz/)
duvet	n	/'duːveɪ/
fan	n	/fæn/
mirror	n	/'mɪrə/ (AmE /'mɪrər/)
pillow	n	/'pɪləʊ/
photos	n	/'fəʊtəʊz/
posters	n	/'pəʊstəz/ (AmE /'pəʊstərz/)
rubbish bin	n	/'rʌbɪʃ bɪn/
shelf	n	/ʃelf/

Unit 3

daily life

clean the floor	phr	/kliːn ðə 'flɔː/ (AmE /flɔːr/)
do the dishes	phr	/duː ðə 'dɪʃɪz/
do the housework	phr	/duː ðə haʊswɜːk/ (AmE /'haʊswɜːrk/)
do the shopping	phr	/duː ðə ʃɒpɪŋ/
do the washing	phr	/duː ðə wɒʃɪŋ/
do the washing up	phr	/duː ðə wɒʃɪŋ ʌp/
lay the table	phr	/leɪ ðə 'teɪbl/
light the fire	phr	/laɪt ðə 'faɪə/ (AmE /faɪr/)
make breakfast	phr	/meɪk 'brekfəst/
make dinner	phr	/meɪk 'dɪnə/ (AmE / meɪk 'dɪnər/)
make the bed	phr	/meɪk ðə 'bed/

other verbs		
admire	v	/əd'maɪə/ (AmE / əd'maɪr/)
survive	v	/sə'vaɪv/ (AmE /sər'vaɪv/)

in the city		
architecture	n	/'ɑːkɪtektʃə/ (AmE /'ɑːrkɪtektʃər/)
attraction	n	/ə'trækʃən/
city centre	n	/'sɪti 'sentə/ (AmE /'sɪti 'sentər/)
concert	n	/'kɒnsət/ (AmE /'kɒnsərt/)
conference	n	/'kɒnfərəns/
cycling track	n	/'saɪklɪŋ 'træk/
district	n	/'dɪstrɪkt/
exhibition centre	n	/eksɪ'bɪʃn 'sentə/ (AmE /eksɪ'bɪʃn 'sentər/)
museum	n	/mju:'ziːəm/
network	n	/'netwɜːk/ (AmE /'netwɜːrk/)
park	n	/pɑːk/ (AmE /pɑːrk/)
passer-by	n	/'pɑːsəbaɪ/ (AmE /'pæsərbaɪ/)
pedestrian	n	/pə'destriən/
playground	n	/'pleɪgraʊnd/
port	n	/pɔːt/ (AmE /pɔːrt/)
square	n	/skweə/ (AmE /skweər/)
stadium	n	/'steɪdiəm/
statue	n	/'stætjuː/
tourist	n	/'tʊərɪst/
tower	n	/'taʊə/ (AmE /'taʊər/)
underground	n	/'ʌndəgraʊnd/ (AmE /'ʌndərgraʊnd/)
visitor	n	/'vɪzɪtə/ (AmE /'vɪzɪtər/)

adjectives		
boring	adj	/'bɔːrɪŋ/
curious	adj	/'kjʊəriəs/
ecological	adj	/iːkə'lɒdʒɪkl/
extraordinary	adj	/ɪks'trɔːdɪnri/
grateful	adj	/'greɪtfl/
healthy	adj	/'helθi/
historic	adj	/hɪs'tɒrɪk/
huge	adj	/hjuːdʒ/
major	adj	/'meɪdʒə/ (AmE /'meɪdʒər/)
narrow	adj	/'nærəʊ/
old-fashioned	adj	/əʊld 'fæʃnd/
respectful	adj	/rɪ'spektfʊl/
shocked	adj	/ʃɒkt/
strange	adj	/streɪndʒ/
striking	adj	/'straɪkɪŋ/

Unit 4

food occasions		
baked fish	n	/beɪkt 'fɪʃ/
bread roll	n	/'bred rəʊl/
chocolate cake	n	/'tʃɒklət keɪk/
green salad	n	/griːn 'sæləd/
lemon tart	n	/lemən 'tɑːt/ (AmE /lemən 'tɑːrt/)
roast chicken	n	/rəʊst 'tʃɪkɪn/
soft drink	n	/'sɒft drɪŋk/
spinach omelette	n	/'spɪnɪtʃ 'ɒmlət/
strawberries and cream	n	/'strɔːbriz ənd 'kriːm/

special occasions		
birthday party	n	/'bɜːθdeɪ pɑːti/ (AmE /'bɜːθdeɪ pɑːrti/)
book	v	/bʊk/
invite	v	/ɪn'vaɪt/
menu	n	/'menjuː/

New Year's Eve	n	/njuː jɪəz 'iːv/ (AmE/njuː jɪərz 'iːv/)
organise	v	/'ɔːgənaɪz/ (AmE /'ɔːrgənaɪz/)
picnic	n	/'pɪknɪk/
restaurant	n	/'restrɒnt/
wedding anniversary	n	/'wedɪŋ ænɪ'vɜːsəri/ (AmE /'wedɪŋ ænɪ'vɜːrsəri/)

food adjectives		
bitter	adj	/'bɪtə/ (AmE /'bɪtər/)
creamy	adj	/'kriːmi/
delicious	adj	/dɪ'lɪʃəs/
disgusting	adj	/dɪs'gʌstɪŋ/
fresh	adj	/freʃ/
salty	adj	/'sɒlti/
simple	adj	/'sɪmpl/
traditional	adj	/trə'dɪʃənəl/

restaurant adjectives		
excellent	adj	/'eksələnt/
fashionable	adj	/'fæʃnəbl/
lively	adj	/'laɪvli/
modern	adj	/'mɒdən/ (AmE /'mɒdərn/)
relaxed	adj	/rɪ'lækst/
slow	adj	/sləʊ/
smart	adj	/smɑːt/ (AmE /smɑːrt/)
stylish	adj	/'staɪlɪʃ/
unfriendly	adj	/ʌn'frendli/

food and restaurant words		
atmosphere	n	/'ætməsfɪə/ (AmE /'ætməsfɪər/)
chef	n	/ʃef/
ingredients	n	/ɪn'griːdiənts/
live music	n	/laɪv 'mjuːzɪk/
serve	v	/sɜːv/ (AmE /sɜːrv/)
service	n	/sɜːvɪs/ (AmE sɜːrvɪs)
waiter	n	/'weɪtə/ (AmE /'weɪtər/)

Unit 5

going to the doctor		
a nasty cough	n	/ə 'nɑːsti 'kɒf/ (AmE /ə 'næsti 'kɒf/)
accident	n	/'æksɪdənt/
be bitten	phr	/bi 'bɪtn/
be painful	phr	/bi 'peɪnfl/
bleed	v	/bliːd/
blood	n	/blʌd/
break an ankle	phr	/breɪk ən 'æŋkl/
cut yourself	phr	/'kʌt yə'self/ (AmE /'kʌt yər'self/)
earache	n	/'ɪəreɪk/
feel sick	v	/fiːl 'sɪk/
have a sore throat	phr	/'hæv ə 'sɔː 'θrəʊt/ (AmE / 'hæv ə 'sɔːr 'θrəʊt/)
injure	v	/'ɪndʒə/ (AmE /'ɪndʒər/)
lie down	v	/laɪ 'daʊn/
painkillers	n	/'peɪnkɪləz/
prescription	n	/prɪs'krɪpʃən/
put a bandage on	phr	/pʊt ə 'bændɪdʒ ɒn/
recover	v	/rɪ'kʌvə/ (AmE /rɪ'kʌvər/)
rest	v	/rest/
scar	n	/skɑː/ (AmE /skɑːr/)
stomach-ache	n	/'stʌməkeɪk/
tablet	n	/'tæblət/
temperature	n	/'temprətʃə/ (AmE /'temprətʃər/)
wound	n	/wuːnd/
X-ray	n	/'eksreɪ/

compound adjectives		
badly-broken	adj	/ˈbædli ˈbrəʊkn/
chocolate-covered	adj	/ˈtʃɒklət ˈkʌvəd/ (AmE /ˈtʃɒklət ˈkʌvərd/)
freshly-squeezed	adj	/ˈfreʃli ˈskwiːzd/
half-eaten	adj	/ˈhɑːf ˈiːtn/ (AmE /ˈhæf ˈiːtn/)
high-fat	adj	/haɪ ˈfæt/
highly-qualified	adj	/ˈhaɪli ˈkwɒlɪfaɪd/
long-lasting	adj	/ˈlɒŋ ˈlɑːstɪŋ/ (AmE /ˈlɒŋ ˈlæstɪŋ/)
low-cost	adj	/ˈləʊ ˈkɒst/
low-fat	adj	/ˈləʊ ˈfæt/
recently qualified	adj	/ˈriːsəntli ˈkwɒlɪfaɪd/
recently-opened	adj	/ˈriːsəntli ˈəʊpənd/
star-shaped	adj	/ˈstɑː ʃeɪpt/ (AmE /ˈstɑːr ʃeɪpt/)
stress-free	adj	/ˈstres friː/
two-kilometre	adj	/ˈtuː kɪˈlɒmɪtə/ (AmE /ˈtuː kɪˈlɒmɪtər/)
well-run	adj	/ˈwel rʌn/

Unit 6

forms of transport		
aeroplane (AmE airplane)	n	/ˈeərəpleɪn/ (AmE /ˈeərpleɪn/)
bicycle	n	/ˈbaɪsɪkl/
boat	n	/bəʊt/
bus	n	/bʌs/
car	n	/kɑː/ (AmE /kɑːr/)
dog sled	n	/ˈdɒg sled/
train	n	/treɪn/

transport words		
announcement	n	/əˈnaʊnsmənt/
baggage	n	/ˈbægɪdʒ/
bike ride	n	/ˈbaɪk raɪd/
board	v	/bɔːd/ (AmE /bɔːrd/)
brakes	n	/breɪks/
cabin	n	/ˈkæbɪn/
carriage	n	/ˈkærɪdʒ/
catch	v	/kætʃ/
check-in	n	/ˈtʃekɪn/
cycle	v	/ˈsaɪkl/
deck	n	/dek/
engine	n	/ˈendʒɪn/
flight	n	/flaɪt/
fuel	n	/fʊəl/
helmet	n	/ˈhelmɪt/
ice	n	/aɪs/
luggage	n	/ˈlʌgɪdʒ/
motor	n	/ˈməʊtə/ (AmE /ˈməʊtər/)
overtake	v	/əʊvəˈteɪk/ (AmE /əʊvərˈteɪk/)
passenger	n	/ˈpæsɪndʒə/ (AmE /ˈpæsɪndʒər/)
platform	n	/ˈplætfɔːm/ (AmE /ˈplætfɔːrm/)
pull	v	/pʊl/
route	n	/ruːt/
sail	v	/seɪl/
seat	n	/siːt/
seat belt	n	/ˈsiːt belt/
skis	n	/skiːz/
snow	n	/snəʊ/
traffic	n	/ˈtræfɪk/
trek	n	/trek/
voyage	n	/ˈvɔɪdʒ/
wave	n	/weɪv/
windscreen (AmE windshield)	n	/ˈwɪndskriːn/ (AmE ˈwɪndʃiːld)

wings	n	/wɪŋz/
yacht	n	/ɒt/

the natural world		
cave	n	/keɪv/
cliff	n	/klɪf/
desert	n	/ˈdezət/ (AmE /ˈdezərt/)
environment	n	/ɪnˈvaɪrəmənt/
expedition	n	/ekspəˈdɪʃn/
forest	n	/ˈfɒrɪst/
lake	n	/leɪk/
mountain	n	/ˈmaʊntɪn/
rainforest	n	/ˈreɪnfɒrɪst/
waterfall	n	/ˈwɔːtəfɔːl/ (AmE /ˈwɔːtərfɔːl/)
wildlife	n	/ˈwaɪldlaɪf/

animals and plants		
branch	n	/brɑːntʃ/ (AmE /bræntʃ/)
bush	n	/bʊʃ/
butterfly	n	/ˈbʌtəflaɪ/ (AmE /ˈbʌtərflaɪ/)
cat	n	/kæt/
crocodile	n	/ˈkrɒkədaɪl/
flower	n	/ˈflaʊə/ (AmE /ˈflaʊər/)
giraffe	n	/dʒɪˈrɑːf/ (AmE /dʒɪˈræf/)
insect	n	/ˈɪnsekt/
leaf	n	/liːf/
monkey	n	/ˈmʌŋki/
parrot	n	/ˈpærət/
polar bear	n	/ˈpəʊlə ˈbeə/ (AmE /ˈpəʊlər ˈbeər/)
snake	n	/sneɪk/
tree	n	/triː/
whale	n	/weɪl/
zebra	n	/ˈzebrə/

adjectives		
dangerous	adj	/ˈdeɪndʒərəs/
peaceful	adj	/ˈpiːsfl/
rare	adj	/reə/ (AmE /reər/)
unknown	adj	/ʌnˈnəʊn/
well-known	adj	/ˈwelnəʊn/
wild	adj	/waɪld/

Unit 7

sports		
climbing	n	/ˈklaɪmɪŋ/
do athletics	phr	/duː æθˈletɪks/
do fencing	phr	/duː ˈfensɪŋ/
do karate	phr	/duː kəˈrɑːti/
go cycling	phr	/gəʊ ˈsaɪklɪŋ/
go horse-riding	phr	/gəʊ ˈhɔːsraɪdɪŋ/ (AmE / gəʊ ˈhɔːrsraɪdɪŋ/)
go running	phr	/gəʊ ˈrʌnɪŋ/
go shooting	phr	/gəʊ ˈʃuːtɪŋ/
go snow boarding	phr	/gəʊ ˈsnəʊbɔːdɪŋ/ (AmE /gəʊ ˈsnəʊbɔːrdɪŋ/)
go swimming	phr	/gəʊ ˈswɪmɪŋ/
go windsurfing	phr	/gəʊ ˈwɪndsɜːfɪŋ/ (AmE /gəʊ ˈwɪnd sɜːrfɪŋ/)
play football	phr	/pleɪ ˈfʊtbɔːl/
play golf	phr	/pleɪ ˈgɒlf/
play hockey	phr	/pleɪ ˈhɒki/
play tennis	phr	/pleɪ ˈtenɪs/
sailing	n	/ˈseɪlɪŋ/
water sports	n	/ˈwɔːtə spɔːts/ (AmE /ˈwɔːtər spɔːrts/)
yachting	n	/ˈjɒtɪŋ/

sports words

ball	*n*	/bɔːl/
boots	*n*	/buːts/
court	*n*	/kɔːt/ (AmE /kɔːrt/)
football (AmE soccer)	*n*	/'fʊtbɔːl/ (AmE /'sɒkər/
glove	*n*	/glʌv/
goal	*n*	/gəʊl/
helmet	*n*	/'helmɪt/
pitch	*n*	/pɪʧ/
racket	*n*	/'rækɪt/
riding school	*n*	/'raɪdɪŋ skuːl/
running shoes	*n*	/'rʌnɪŋ ʃuːz/
shooting range	*n*	/'ʃuːtɪŋ reɪnʤ/
shorts	*n*	/ʃɔːts/ (AmE /ʃɔːrts/)
swimming pool	*n*	/'swɪmɪŋ puːl/
swimsuit	*n*	/'swɪmsuːt/
target	*n*	/'tɑːgɪt/ (AmE /tɑːrgɪt/)
track	*n*	/træk/
uniform	*n*	/'juːnɪfɔːm/ (AmE /'juːnɪfɔːrm/)

feelings and opinions

be amazed	*phr*	/biː ə'meɪzd/
be anxious	*phr*	/biː 'æŋkʃəs/
be certain	*phr*	/biː 'sɜːtən/ (AmE /biː 'sɜːrtən/)
be confident	*phr*	/biː 'kɒnfɪdənt/
be disappointed	*phr*	/biː dɪsə'pɔɪntɪd/
be jealous	*phr*	/biː 'ʤeləs/
be nervous	*phr*	/biː 'nɜːvəs/ (AmE /biː 'nɜːrvəs/)
be pleased	*phr*	/biː pliːzd/
be proud of someone	*phr*	/biː 'praʊd əv 'sʌmwʌn/
be surprised	*phr*	/biː sə'praɪzd/ (AmE /biː sər'praɪzd/)
be upset	*phr*	/biː ʌp'set/

competitions

competition	*n*	/kɒmpə'tɪʃn/
final	*n*	/'faɪnl/
prize	*n*	/praɪz/
result	*n*	/rɪ'zʌlt/
success	*n*	/sʌk'ses/
take part	*v*	/teɪk 'pɑːt/ (AmE /teɪk 'pɑːrt/)
win	*v*	/wɪn/

Unit 8

school and study

certificate	*n*	/sə'tɪfɪkət/ (AmE /sər'tɪfɪkət/)
classroom	*n*	/'klɑːsruːm/ (AmE /'klæsruːm/)
college	*n*	/'kɒlɪʤ/
corridor	*n*	/'kɒrɪdɔː/ (AmE /'kɒrɪdɔːr/)
curriculum	*n*	/kə'rɪkjʊlʌm/
degree	*n*	/dɪ'griː/
diploma	*n*	/dɪ'pləʊmə/
education	*n*	/edjuː'keɪʃn/
essay	*n*	/'eseɪ/
fail an exam	*phr*	/'feɪl ən ɪg'zæm/
homework	*n*	/'həʊmwɜːk/ (AmE /'həʊmwɜːrk/)
laboratory	*n*	/lə'bɒrətri/ (AmE /'læbrətɔːri/)
lessons	*n*	/'lesnz/
library	*n*	/'laɪbri/ (AmE /'laɪbrəri/)
lost property	*n*	/lɒst 'prɒpəti/ (AmE /lɒst 'prɒpərti/)
packed lunch	*n*	/pækt 'lʌntʃ/
pass an exam	*phr*	/'pɑːs ən ɪg'zæm/ (AmE /'pæs ən ɪg'zæm/)
permission	*n*	/pə'mɪʃn/ (AmE /pər'mɪʃn/)
project	*n*	/'prɒʤekt/
punishment	*n*	/'pʌnɪʃmənt/
qualification	*n*	/kwɒlɪfɪ'keɪʃn/
rule	*n*	/ruːl/
school	*n*	/skuːl/
spending money	*n*	/'spendɪŋ 'mʌni/
subject	*n*	/'sʌbʤekt/
take an exam	*phr*	/'teɪk ən ɪg'zæm/
timetable	*n*	/'taɪmteɪbl/
university	*n*	/juːnɪ'vɜːsɪti/ (AmE /juːnɪ'vɜːrsɪti/)

jobs

actor	*n*	/'æktə/ (AmE /'æktər/)
babysitter	*n*	/'beɪbi'sɪtə/ (AmE /'beɪbi'sɪtər/)
basketball player	*n*	/'bɑːskɪtbɔːl pleɪə/ (AmE 'bæskɪtbɔːl pleɪər/)
chef	*n*	/ʃef/
dogwalker	*n*	/'dɒg 'wɒːkə/ (AmE /'dɒːg 'wɒːkər/)
flight attendant	*n*	/'flaɪt ə'tendənt/
football coach	*n*	/'fʊtbɔːl kəʊʧ/
instructor	*n*	/ɪn'strʌktə/ (AmE /ɪn'strʌktər/)
journalist	*n*	/'ʤɜːnəlɪst/ (AmE /'ʤɜːrnəlɪst/)
musician	*n*	/mjuː'zɪʃn/
scientist	*n*	/'saɪəntɪst/
shop assistant (AmE salesclerk)	*n*	/ʃɒːp ə'sɪstənt/ (AmE /'seɪlzklɑːk/)
video game writer	*n*	/'vɪdiəʊ geɪm raɪtə/ (AmE /'vɪdiəʊ geɪm raɪtər/)
waiter	*n*	/weɪtə/ (AmE /weɪtər/)

job words

company	*n*	/'kʌmpəni/
conference	*n*	/'kɒnfərəns/
CV	*n*	/siː'viː/
experience	*n*	/ɪk'spɪəriəns/
interview	*n*	/'ɪntəvjuː/ (AmE /'ɪntərvjuː/)
job	*n*	/ʤɒb/
job advertisement	*n*	/'ʤɒb əd'vɜːtɪsmənt/ (AmE /ʤɒb əd'vɜːrtɪsmənt/)
letter of application	*n*	/'letər əv æplɪ'keɪʃn/
part-time job	*n*	/'pɑːt taɪm ʤɒb/ (AmE /'pɑːrt taɪm ʤɒb/)
pay	*n*	/peɪ/
qualification	*n*	/kwɒlɪfɪ'keɪʃn/
training	*n*	/'treɪnɪŋ/

Unit 9

computers and technology

camera	*n*	/'kæmrə/
chip	*n*	/ʧɪp/
computer	*n*	/kəm'pjuːtə/ (AmE /kəm'pjuːtər/)
digital	*adj*	/'dɪʤɪtl/
display	*v*	/dɪs'pleɪ/
fridge	*n*	/frɪʤ/
heating	*n*	/'hiːtɪŋ/
interactive	*adj*	/ɪntə'ræktɪv/
lights	*n*	/laɪts/
network	*n*	/'netwɜːk/ (AmE /'netwɜːrk/)
product	*n*	/'prɒdʌkt/
program	*n*	/'prəʊgræm/
refrigerator	*n*	/rɪ'frɪʤəreɪtə/ (AmE /rɪ'frɪʤəreɪtər/)
remote control	*n*	/rɪ'məʊt kən'trəʊl/
robot	*n*	/'rəʊbɒt/
software	*n*	/'sɒftweə/ (AmE /'sɑːftweər/)
switch off	*v*	/swɪʧ 'ɒf/
system	*n*	/'sɪstəm/

weather

weather		
climate	n	/'klaɪmət/
disappear	v	/dɪsə'pɪə/ (AmE /dɪsə'pɪər/)
drought	n	/draʊt/
gales	n	/geɪlz/
global warming	n	/'gləʊbəl 'wɔːmɪŋ/ (AmE /'gləʊbəl 'wɔːrmɪŋ/)
heavy rain	n	/'hevi reɪn/
high temperatures	phr	/'haɪ 'temprɪtʃəz/ (AmE /'haɪ 'temprɪtʃərz/)
hot summers	phr	/'hɒt 'sʌməz/ (AmE /'hɒt 'sʌmərz/)
ice	n	/aɪs/
increase	v	/'ɪnkriːs/
lack of rain	phr	/'læk əv 'reɪn/
lightning	n	/'laɪtnɪŋ/
low temperatures	phr	/'ləʊ 'temprɪtʃəz/ (AmE /'ləʊ 'temprɪtʃərz/)
mild winters	phr	/'maɪld 'wɪntəz/ (AmE /'maɪld 'wɪntərz/)
reduce	v	/rɪ'djuːs/
rise	v	/raɪz/
snow	n	/snəʊ/
storm	n	/stɔːm/ (AmE /stɔːrm/)
take action	v	/teɪk 'ækʃn/
thunder	n	/'θʌndə/ (AmE /'θʌndər/)
tropical storm	n	/'trɒpɪkl 'stɔːm/ (AmE /'trɒpɪkl 'stɔːrm/)
wildfires	n	/'waɪldfaɪəz/ (AmE /'waɪldfaɪrz/)

Unit 10

holidays

holidays		
art gallery	n	/'ɑːt 'gæləri/ (AmE /'ɑːrt 'gæləri/)
beach	n	/biːtʃ/
cathedral	n	/kə'θiːdrəl/
cruise	n	/kruːz/
diving	n	/'daɪvɪŋ/
do something challenging	phr	/'duː 'sʌmθɪŋ 'tʃælɪndʒɪŋ/
enjoy beautiful scenery	phr	/ɪn'dʒɔɪ 'bjuːtɪfl 'siːnəri/
have fun	phr	/hæv 'fʌn/
learn a new skill	phr	/'lɜːn ə njuː 'skɪl/ (AmE /'lɜːrn ə njuː 'skɪl/)
learn about new places	phr	/'lɜːn əbaʊt 'njuː 'pleɪsɪz/ (AmE /'lɜːrn əbaʊt 'njuː 'pleɪsɪz/)
look at famous buildings	phr	/'lʊk ət 'feɪməs 'bɪldɪŋz/
monument	n	/'mɒnjʊmənt/
museum	n	/mjuː'ziːəm/
relax	v	/rɪ'læks/
sightseeing	n	/'saɪtsiːɪŋ/
souvenir shop	n	/suːvə'nɪə ʃɒp/ (AmE /suːvə'nɪər ʃɑːp/)
travel agent	n	/'trævl 'eɪdʒənt/
trip	n	/trɪp/

music and festivals

music and festivals		
drum n' bass	n	/'drʌm ən 'beɪs/
electronic	adj	/elɪk'trɒnɪk/
folk	adj	/fəʊk/
hiphop	adj	/'hɪphɒp/
indie	adj	/'ɪndi/
rock	adj	/rɒk/

places to stay

places to stay		
campsite	n	/'kæmpsaɪt/
guesthouse	n	/'gesthaʊs/
hotel	n	/həʊ'tel/

forms of entertainment

forms of entertainment		
comedy	n	/'kɒmədi/
drumming lesson	n	/'drʌmɪŋ 'lesn/
fancy dress competition	n	/'fænsi 'dres kɒmpə'tɪʃn/
funfair	n	/'fʌnfeə/ (AmE /'fʌnfeər/)
performance	n	/pə'fɔːməns/ (AmE /pər'fɔːrməns/)
poetry reading	n	/'pəʊətri 'riːdɪŋ/
puppet show	n	/'pʌpɪt ʃəʊ/
stage show	n	/'steɪdʒ ʃəʊ/
stalls	n	/stɔːlz/
theatre	n	/'θɪətə/ (AmE /'θɪətər/)
zoo	n	/zuː/

Unit 11

clothes

clothes		
belt	n	/belt/
boots	n	/buːts/
coat	n	/kəʊt/
dress	n	/dres/
gloves	n	/glʌvz/
handbag	n	/'hændbæg/
high heels	n	/'haɪ 'hiːlz/
jeans	n	/dʒiːnz/
jumper (AmE sweater)	n	/'dʒʌmpə/ (AmE /'swetər/
pyjamas	n	/pə'dʒɑːməz/ (AmE /pə'dʒæməz/)
shirt	n	/ʃɜːt/ (AmE /ʃɜːrt/)
shorts	n	/ʃɔːts/ (AmE /ʃɔːrts/)
skirt	n	/skɜːt/ (AmE /skɜːrt/)
socks	n	/sɒks/
T-shirt	n	/'tiːʃɜːt/ (AmE /'tiːʃɜːrt/)
top	n	/'tɒp/ (AmE /tɑːp/)
trainers (AmE sneakers)	n	/'treɪnəz/ (AmE /'sniːkərz/)
trousers (AmE pants)	n	/'traʊzəz/ (AmE /pænts/)

adjectives describing clothes

adjectives describing clothes		
blue	adj	/bluː/
bright	adj	/braɪt/
brown	adj	/braʊn/
cotton	adj	/'kɒtn/
denim	adj	/denɪm/
designer	adj	/dɪ'zaɪnə/ (AmE /dɪ'zaɪnər/)
leather	adj	/'leðə/ (AmE /'leðər/)
orange	adj	/'ɒrɪndʒ/
pale	adj	/peɪl/
patterned	adj	/'pætənd/ (AmE /'pætərnd/)
plastic	adj	/'plæstɪk/
pretty	adj	/'prɪti/
red	adj	/red/
short	adj	/ʃɔːt/ (AmE /ʃɔːrt/)
silk	adj	/sɪlk/
sporty	adj	/'spɔːti/ (AmE /'spɔːrti/)
trendy	adj	/'trendi/
ugly	adj	/'ʌgli/
white	adj	/waɪt/

money		
afford	v	/əˈfɔːd/ (AmE /əˈfɔːrd/)
bill	n	/bɪl/
cash	n	/kæʃ/
credit card	n	/ˈkredɪt kɑːd/ (AmE /ˈkredɪt kɑːrd/)
discount	n	/ˈdɪskaʊnt/
exchange	v	/ˈɪksˈtʃeɪndʒ/
pay the full price	phr	/ˈpeɪ ðə fʊl ˈpraɪs/
receipt	n	/rɪˈsiːt/
take something back	phr	/ˈteɪk sʌmθɪŋ ˈbæk/
tip	n	/tɪp/

Unit 12

the cinema		
action	n	/ˈækʃn/
adventure	n	/ədˈventʃə/ (AmE /ədˈventʃər/)
advertisement	n	/ədˈvɜːtɪsmənt/ (AmE /ədˈvɜːrtɪsmənt/)
animation	n	/ænɪˈmeɪʃn/
audience	n	/ˈɔːdiəns/
character	n	/ˈkærɪktə/ (AmE /ˈkærɪktər/)
comedy	n	/ˈkɒmədi/
curtain	n	/ˈkɜːtn/ (AmE /ˈkɜːrtn/)
fantasy	n	/ˈfæntəsi/
film director	n	/fɪlm daɪˈrektə/ (AmE /fɪlm daɪˈrektər/)
historical drama	n	/hɪsˈtɒrɪkl ˈdrɑːmə/ (AmE /hɪsˈtɒrɪkl ˈdræmə/)
musical	n	/ˈmjuːzɪkl/
performance	n	/pəˈfɔːməns/ (AmE /pərˈfɔːrməns/)
popcorn	n	/ˈpɒpkɔːn/ (AmE /ˈpɒpkɔːrn/)
romance	n	/ˈrəʊmæns/
row	n	/rəʊ/
scene	n	/siːn/
science fiction	n	/ˈsaɪəns ˈfɪkʃn/
screen	n	/skriːn/
seat	n	/siːt/
special effects	n	/ˈspeʃəl ɪˈfekts/
star	n	/stɑː/ (AmE /stɑːr/)
thriller	n	/ˈθrɪlə/ (AmE /ˈθrɪlər/)
ticket	n	/ˈtɪkɪt/

reporting verbs		
ask	v	/ɑːsk/ (AmE /æsk/)
explain	v	/ɪksˈpleɪn/
persuade	v	/pəˈsweɪd/ (AmE /pərˈsweɪd/)
promise	v	/ˈprɒmɪs/
say	v	/seɪ/
suggest	v	/səˈdʒest/
tell	v	/tel/
warn	v	/wɔːn/ (AmE /wɔːrn/)

CAMBRIDGE UNIVERSITY PRESS
www.cambridge.org/elt

RICHMOND PUBLISHING
www.richmondelt.com

© Richmond Publishing 2010
(PET *Direct* was originally published by Richmond
Publishing as *Target PET* © Richmond Publishing 2009)

Printed in Spain
Depósito legal: M-22125-2013

ISBN 978-0-521-16711-6 Student's Book with CD-ROM
ISBN 978-0-521-16714-7 Workbook without answers
ISBN 978-0-521-16715-4 Workbook with answers
ISBN 978-0-521-16716-1 Teacher's Book with Class Audio CD
ISBN 978-0-521-16722-2 Student's Pack (*Student's Book with
CD-ROM and Workbook without answers*)

Acknowledgments:

Publisher: Deborah Tricker
Commissioning Editor: Matthew Duffy
Development Editor: Imogen Wyllie
Proofreader: Karen White
Design and Layout: Rob Briggs, Dave Kuzmicki
Cover Design: Georgie French
Photo Research: Magdalena Mayo
Audio Production: Paul Ruben Productions, Inc. NYC
Legal consulting and copyright clearance: Ruz Legal,
Spain

Publisher acknowledgements:
The publishers would like to thank the following
reviewers for their valuable feedback which has made
this project possible.

Elizabeth Beck (Italy), Gertrude Baxter (Universad
Tecnologica de la Mixteca, Mexico), Claudia Bonilla
Cassani (Colegio del Tepeyac, Mexico), Maria
Consuelo Velasco (Colombia), Karen Dyer (Madrid,
Spain), Melissa Ferrin (Universad Tecnologica de
la Mixteca, Mexico), Angieszka Gugnacka-Cook
(ELC Łódź, Poland), Andrea Harries (The English
Company, Colombia), Analía Kandel (Argentina),
Gabby Maguire (International House Barcelona, Spain),
Roberta Natalini (Intuition Languages-IH, UK), Laura
Renart (ISP Dr Sáenz, Universad Virtual de Quilmes,
Argentina), Agnieszka Tyszkiewicz-Zora (ELC Łódź,
Poland)

The publishers would also like to thank all those who
have given their kind permission to reproduce or adapt
material for this book.

Texts:
p 25 "Shark attacks boy in his bedroom"
© Expressandstar.com All rights reserved

p. 74 "School of rock" © Telegraph.co.uk. All rights
reserved

*Every effort has been made to trace the holders of
copyright before publication. The publishers will be
pleased to rectify any error or omission at the earliest
opportunity.*

Illustrations:
Charlene Chua, Scott Garrett, Aleix Pons Oliver,
Colin Shelbourn, Terry Wong

Photographs:
D. Lezama; J. Jaime; J. M.ª Escudero/Instituto
Municipal de Deportes de Madrid; Prats i Camps;
S. Enríquez; A. G. E. FOTOSTOCK; ACI AGENCIA DE
FOTOGRAFÍA/Alamy Images; COMSTOCK; CORDON
PRESS/CORBIS/Zefa/Judith Wagner, Ariel Skelley,
Zefa/B. Bird; COVER/Creatas Images, CORBIS;
DIGITALVISION; FOTONONSTOP/Vincent Leblic; GETTY
IMAGES SALES SPAIN/Stewart Cohen, Taxi/Philip Lee
Harvey, Kevin Summers, Tetra Images, Stone/Rich
Iwasaki, Stone/Jerome Tisne, Joe McDonald, Blake
Little, Steven Miric, Stone/DreamPictures, Dougal
Waters, AFP PHOTO/Carl de Souza, Siri Stafford,
Photodisc/SW Productions, Digital Vision, Taxi/Zubin
Shroff, Ian O'Leary, Ian Cumming, Stone/Don Klumpp,
Riser/Martin San, Sean Ellis, Panoramic Images,
Taxi/Tara Moore, DMH Images, Adina Tovy, Werner
Dieterich, Stone/Bruce Ayres, The Image Bank/Yellow
Dog Productions, Iconica/Antonio Mo, Riser/Marco
Simoni, Stone/Brian Bailey, Blend Images/John Lund/
Sam Diephuis, Win-Initiative, Taxi/Tony Hopewell,
Lifesize/Paul Burns, Riser/Rapsodia, Stone/Robert
Frerck, Stone/Britt Erlanson, Iconica/John Giustina,
Richard Nowitz, Stockbyte, Photodisc/Siri Stafford,
Iconica/Jose Luis Pelaez, The Image Bank/Luis
Castaneda, The Image Bank/John Eder, Blend Images/
Klaus Tiedge, Digital Vision/Paul Burns, The Image
Bank/Peter Lilja, Red Chopsticks, Riser/Christopher
Bissell, Frank and Helena Herholdt, Iconica/Philip
and Karen Smith, The Image Bank/Simon Wilkinson,
Ghislain & Marie David de Lossy, Digital Vision/
Lecorre Productions, R and R Images, Mike Kemp,
Mike Harrington; HIGHRES PRESS STOCK/AbleStock.
com; ISTOCKPHOTO; PHOTODISC; Daniel Rozados;
wishlist images; Harrods; MATTON-BILD; SERIDEC
PHOTOIMAGENES CD; ARCHIVO SANTILLANA